Meditation and Yoga Fundamentals

*The Essential Guide to Learn
Meditation Techniques, Yoga
breathing Techniques, Relieve
Stress and Manage Anxiety*

2 Manuscripts in 1 book

Mark Gabriel Reynolds

This book set includes:
-Meditation and Mantras for beginners
-Pranayama breathing techniques book

Introduction to meditation

Are you facing the stresses of modern-day life? Do you often lie awake all night with anxious thoughts racing through your mind? Have you been paying more attention to the trending topics about meditation lately? If yes, you probably wonder why so many people are talking about the benefits of meditation and the emergence of meditation studios, classes, and podcasts. Due to our increasingly stressful lives - mental health has never been spoken so publicly about.

Meditation is a practice where a person uses a series of techniques, like mindfulness - to focus their thoughts and mind on an activity, thought, or object to train their awareness and attention. The goal behind this is to help a person achieve clear-headedness and an emotionally calm and stable state. When this state is achieved, they are able to achieve better sleep, mental health, and higher levels of relaxation.

A common misunderstanding of meditation is that people think that it sounds "easy." It isn't. You may even currently be thinking, 'how hard can it be to just sit there and not think?'. This is actually more difficult than it sounds as humans are very used to always thinking and worrying about something. This is due to the neural pathways in our brain that's been imprinted there to cause us to consciously think and worry about topics that may not be an actual threat to us. Learning how to perform meditation correctly will help you better grasp what your thoughts actually are, which helps provide you with a sense of calm. When you understand your own feelings, emotions, and thoughts, you will better be able to manage your own behavior.

With the meditation trends that are happening in the current day, you may think that listening to a meditation podcast or going to a meditation class once a week will benefit you. These types of meditation won't help you make the lasting changes that you'll need to cope with your daily stresses and anxieties. Sure, the voice of the meditation podcast you regularly frequent may sound very relaxing and always has a charming British accent - but ultimately, you've forgotten everything it has said to you the moment your foot is out the door. In this book, I will help you navigate the different types of meditation, mantras, and transcripts that will help you achieve the discipline and strategy to incorporate meditation and mindfulness into your lifestyle.

Learning how to meditate effectively will help you achieve greater mindfulness, which prevents unhealthy and anxious thoughts from racing through your head 24 hours of the day. A common goal in meditation is to achieve mindfulness, which has been proven to decrease a person's stress, anxiety, and insomnia. This book will cover topics that will help you understand the benefits meditation will bring into your life and learn about the different types of meditation that can help you with problems related to sleep, anxiety, and relaxation. I will teach you how to practice meditation every day, including information on building good meditation habits and building a routine for yourself.

This book contains topics that will help you learn how to combat your own psychological challenges that may be affecting your day to day life. You will learn the simplest form of meditation all the way to incorporating meditation in all your day to day activities. You will begin to understand how meditation will help you begin the process of loving yourself and letting go of negative thoughts. You will be able to achieve a non-judgmental state of mind that will free your mind to accept everybody.

Part 1

Chapter 1: A History of Meditation

Let's start off by learning a little about the history of meditation. The first written evidence of meditation was first seen in the Vedas in 1500 BCE. The Vedas are a collection of ancient religious texts and hymns written in India between 1500 and 1000 BCE. This means that meditation was first developed in India. In India, there is a tradition of *Guru and Shishya,* which is the modern-day equivalent of teacher and disciple. Students of this tradition were sent to schools that were located in forests to learn and live under a successful teacher. During this time, people passed on all of the learning and knowledge on this topic through word of mouth. It's obvious to say that we're not able to dedicate our lives to a Guru and move into the middle of a forest and study meditation under intense training in the modern-day. Most of us don't even live near forests! Over the last thousands of years, meditation has changed into something that everyone can do comfortably in their own homes and at their own pace. Meditation has become easily accessible, and you don't need your own Guru to learn it.

What Is Meditation?

In today's modern world, many misconceptions come to mind when you think of mindfulness and meditation. Many people think that meditation is a person sitting cross-legged and chanting a mantra or that it is something that monks do in movies. These are common myths that actually have nothing to do with actual meditation and mindfulness. In fact, you can practice mindfulness while washing the dishes, and nobody would know that you were 'meditating.' Mindfulness and meditation can come in many different forms, whether it's the act of meditating during a yoga session or if it's a prescribed course of cognitive-behavioral therapy. Mindfulness is a part of many different exercises and techniques to help people live happier lives.

Let's first learn the basics of mindfulness and meditation. Mindfulness is most popularly achieved through the use of meditation. What exactly does this entail? Pema Chodron says a famous quote: "Meditation is a process of lightening up, of trusting the basic goodness of what we have and who we are, and of realizing that any wisdom that exists, exists in what we already have. We can lead our life so as to become more awake to who we are and what we're doing rather than trying to improve or change or get rid of who we are or what we're doing. The key is to wake up, to become more alert, more inquisitive and curious about ourselves."

This quote helps describe meditation in its purest form. In our society today, psychology professionals describe meditation as a way to achieve mindfulness. Mindfulness is then described as a method of focusing one's thoughts and mind on an activity, thought, or object to train their awareness and attention. The goal of this is to help the person achieve clear-headedness and an emotionally calm and stable state. You may think that mindfulness sounds easy just by reading what it is, but it actually is difficult to achieve. Mindfulness is something that requires strong self-discipline to achieve, and simply just listening to a mindfulness podcast or going to one mindfulness class isn't going to help you become a mindful person.

What Does Meditation Mean to You?

Each person reading this book has a different reason that brought them here. Each person's reasoning as to why they want to learn how to become mindful will vary slightly, but the root of everyone's reasons are the same; you want to change your life for the better!

If you are unsure of your motive or your "why," take some time to look deep within yourself and address the reasons why you are reading this book or the reasons why you feel it is time to make a change in your life. By taking stock of your feelings, will lead you to find your motivation for seeking change. Whatever your objective, writing it down will help to solidify it and make it more real. By having it written down on paper, you will have put your reason for doing all of this out into the universe, and it will make you feel as if there is no going back now. This will keep you motivated when times get tough. You can revisit that paper anytime you need a reminder of why you are taking on such a challenge. Seeing that paper will remind you of why it is all worth it.

Understanding the specific reasons you want to learn mindfulness and meditation will be the most important part of your journey. This is because having a strong reason *why* will keep you motivated, even when the process is difficult.

Take some time before continuing to find out your reasons for seeking this book in the first place. Are you learning to meditate because you are under a lot of stress? Did your therapist recommend meditation to help with your anxiety? Do you simply want to do this to find more peace in your day to day life?

Meditation Vs. Mindfulness

Mindfulness is only one type of meditation, but it is one of the most basic types of meditation you need to learn before moving on to other types. Mindfulness helps you become aware of your body and your thoughts. Becoming mindful of your physical body is just as important as being mindful mentally. We do many activities on a daily basis using our bodies that we don't think about, which causes us to lose mindfulness. Have you ever felt yourself go into autopilot while driving to work? Or going into autopilot when you're waiting in a line? These are common things that the human body naturally does to help us save energy throughout the day. To improve our mindfulness, we must overcome our natural tendencies to go into autopilot when we are doing tasks that our body is habitually used to. This chapter will learn about how to be mindful with your observation, commuting, and working. These are three aspects that everyone experiences constantly in their life. I will also teach you about being mindful of your own physical health by paying attention to the activities and foods you are giving to your body. Learning to be more mindful of your own health will not only help you live a healthier life it will also teach you to be more mindful and add value to your goal of mindfulness.

One of the first areas of mindfulness you need to learn is how to conduct mindful observation. Achieving mindful observation is incredibly powerful because it helps you become more aware and appreciate your environment's simple elements in a more profound way. There are a lot of beautiful aspects in our life that we tend to overlook just because our mind is used to them. By achieving mindful observation, you can find simple joys in life, such as; a sunny day, the smell of freshly cut grass, or the soft fur of your cat. Over time, many people who haven't achieved mindful observation tend to become resentful of the place where they reside. For example, they may only begin to notice the bad parts of the apartment they are living in instead of noticing the good. In human nature, it is easy for what is good to become your norm, which takes away from its beauty.

Let's try a mindful observation exercise.

1. Choose a natural object within your current environment and focus on just watching it for a couple of minutes. This could be a plant or an insect, or even the clouds or the moon.
2. Don't do anything else except notice the object you are watching. Simply relax and watch it for long as your concentration will let you.
3. Look at this object as if you are seeing it for the first time.

4. Explore this object visually by focusing on its formation, and allow yourself to be consumed by its presence.
5. Allow yourself to connect with its energy and its natural purpose in the world.

Improving your mindful observation is important to help us better cope with difficult thoughts and feelings that cause us stress and anxiety. By cultivating the moment-by-moment awareness in our surroundings, we achieve mindful observation. If we regularly practice mindfulness meditations, we will harness the ability to anchor the mind in the present moment instead of being influenced by negative experiences of the past and fears of the future. When we master this, we will be able to deal with life's challenges in a clear-minded and calm way.

Being mindful of your physical health is just as important as practicing meditation. If you are unable to pay attention to what you are putting your body through, you are actually affecting your overall mindfulness. People who regularly participate in unhealthy activities like drinking alcohol, smoking, and infrequent exercising are actually fueling their autopilot function to serve instant gratification. Learning to pay attention to your physical health will help you realize that certain unhealthy activities you're used to that make you 'feel good' don't actually make you feel good. We know that practicing mindfulness helps people decrease feelings of stress, anxiety, and depression. Here are some other areas that bring mindful of your physical health can help with:

- **Stress reduction:** When a person is suffering from a lot of stress, it intensifies their depression or anxiety and increases their risk of developing more serious depression or anxiety disorders. Try to make changes in your life that can help you reduce or manage stress. Identify which aspects of your life creates the most stress, such as unhealthy relationships or work overload, and find ways to minimize their impact and the stress it brings.

- **Exercise:** Researchers have found that regularly exercising can be just as effective as medication when it comes to treating depression and anxiety. Exercise boosts the 'feel-good' brain chemicals in the brain such as serotonin and endorphins. These chemicals also trigger the growth of new brain cells and connections similar to what antidepressants do. The best part about exercise is that you don't need to do it intensely in order to have the benefits. Even a simple 30-minute walk can make a huge difference in a person's brain activity. For the best results, people should aim to do 30 – 60 minutes of aerobic activity every day or on most days.

- **Nutrition:** The ability to eat properly is imperative for everyone's mental and physical health. By eating small meals that are well-balanced throughout the day, you can minimize your mood swings and keep your energy levels up. Although you may crave sugary foods due to the quick boost of energy that they can bring, complex carbohydrates are much more nutritious. Instead, complex carbohydrates can provide you with an energy boost without a crash at the end.

- **Social Support:** Having a strong social network reduces isolation, which is a huge risk factor in depression and anxiety. Make an effort to keep in regular contact with family and friends (ideally on a daily basis) and consider joining a support group or class. You can also opt to do some volunteering where you can get the social support you need while helping others as well.

- **Sleep:** A person's sleep cycle has strong effects on mood. When a person does not get enough sleep, their symptoms of depression or anxiety may get worse. Sleep deprivation causes other negative symptoms like sadness, fatigue, moodiness, and irritability. Not many people can function well with less than seven hours of sleep per night. A healthy adult should be aiming for 7 – 9 hours of sleep every night.

Chapter 2: Meditation Examples

We are used to seeing meditation through movies and television, and they all look a little bit silly. However, there are actually so many different types of meditation that hundreds of different postures and stances exist for each and every type. This chapter will be learning about the most common and useful meditation practices that will help you better manage any problems related to sleep, anxiety, relaxation, and breathing. Practicing different types of meditation produces different results. For instance, the Metta meditation helps people generate kindness for themselves, which will help improve their mental wellbeing. However, other meditations focus on spirituality, which may help you in a different way if you are pursuing spiritual enlightenment. We will explore a few different types of meditation in this chapter.

Mindfulness Meditation

The first type of meditation and the most commonly practiced is something called mindfulness meditation. This type of meditation is a type of mental training that helps you to focus on your thoughts as they come by, and the physical sensations that you are experiencing in that moment. This includes your current emotions, physical sensations, and passing thoughts. Mindfulness meditation will help you better cope with mental aspects of your life, such as managing anxiety, depression, pain, and addictions. Scientific based speaking therapies like Cognitive Behavioral Therapy incorporates numerous aspects of mindfulness meditation into their program.

Mindfulness meditation usually involves practicing intentional breathing, using mental images, and developing an awareness of your mind and body. It also involves body relaxation techniques. It is typically easier for beginners to follow a guided meditation directing them throughout the whole process. It is extremely easy to drift away or fall asleep while in meditation if there is nobody guiding you. Once you become more skilled in mindfulness meditation, you are able to do it without a vocal guide, but this requires strong mental capabilities.

Next, we will discuss how to practice mindfulness meditation. An original player in mindfulness practice is called the Mindfulness-Based Stress Reduction (MSBR) technique. This technique is a standardized program within mindfulness meditation.

This program was created by someone called Jon-Kabat-Zinn, Ph.D. He used to be a pupil of a very famous Buddhist monk, *Thich Nhat Hanh*. This particular standardized program focuses on your own awareness and bringing your attention to the present. This method is now being introduced in medical environments to help treat many health conditions, including stress, pain, and insomnia.

This method is fairly straight forward; however, it is recommended that a teacher or program can help guide you as you start. Most people do it for at least ten minutes a day, but even a short practice every single day is proven to help your overall wellbeing. This is the basic technique that will help you get started:

1. Find a quiet place that you feel comfortable in. Ideally, your home or someone where you feel safe. Sit on a chair, or wherever you feel comfortable. Make sure your spine is straight but not tense.

2. Begin trying to sort your thoughts and put aside those that are of the past and future. Stick to the thoughts about the present.

3. Bring your awareness to your breath. Make sure to focus on the feeling and sensation of air moving through your body as you inhale and exhale. Feel the way your belly rises and falls. Feel the air as it enters your nose and leaves again through the mouth. Make sure to notice the differences between each breath.

4. Watch every thought come and go. Act as if you are watching the clouds, letting them pass by you as you watch each one. Whether your thought is a fear, a worry, an anxious thought, or a hope - when these thoughts arise, do not ignore them or try to push them away. Simply acknowledge them, try to stay calm, and anchor yourself with your breaths.

5. You may find yourself getting carried away in your thoughts. If this happens, observe where your mind went off to, and without making a judgment, simply return to your breathing. Keep in mind that this happens a lot with beginners;

try not to be too hard on yourself when this happens. Always use your breathing as an anchor again.

6. As we near the end of the 10-minute session, sit for a couple of minutes and notice again where you physically are. Stand up slowly and gradually.

This is the most standard and basic technique in practicing mindfulness meditation. However, you don't necessarily need to drop everything you're doing to practice this technique. Your daily life actually gives you plenty of opportunities to practice this. Here are a couple of common opportunities that will give you the time you need to practice your meditation.

1. Doing the dishes:
This is a great opportunity to practice meditation as typically nobody will disturb you while you are washing the dishes. This perfect mix between time alone and doing an activity makes a great window to try mindfulness. Try to savor the feeling of warm water on your hands, the feeling of the bubbles, the smell of dish soap, and the sound of pots and pans clunking under the water. Buddhist monk Thich Nhat Hanh named this, "washing the dishes to wash the dishes" instead of rushing through it to move onto the next activity, like watching your favorite TV show or play a video

game. If you're able to give yourself over to this experience, you'll end up with a refreshed mind and clean dishes!

2. Brushing your teeth:
Every single day, you have to brush your teeth - this makes the normally boring task of dental hygiene a chance for you to practice mindfulness. Start by feeling your feet on the ground, toothbrush in hand, and the movement of your arm as you brush your teeth back and forth. One helpful tip is to pretend that there is a scanner - and that it is scanning your body from your feet up. Make sure to focus on each body part as the scanner moves from your feet to your head.

3. Driving:
It is extremely easy for people to become mindless while driving. Especially if you're driving the same route day in and day out, if you're driving to and from work, your mind typically wanders off to what work tasks are needed to be done that day and the chores that you have to come home to once the day is over. Practice your mindfulness in the car as you're driving to keep yourself anchored inside the car. Try to take in what's around you, like the color of the car in front of you. The smell of the inside of your car. The way the steering wheel

fits in your hands. Pay attention to all the noises you hear, from the music on the car radio to the outside traffic noises. Whenever you find yourself wandering, return your attention to the present moment.

4. Exercising:
Make your fitness routines and exercise in mindfulness by exercising without screens and music by focusing on your breathing and where your feet are in the space as you are moving. Sure, watching TV or listening to a podcast will make your run on the treadmill go by faster, but it will not help you to train the mind. Really allow yourself to feel the burn in your muscles and pay attention to how your body reacts to the workout you are putting it through. Don't just ignore a muscle's pain; acknowledge it and really let yourself feel the exercise.

5. Bedtime:
This is usually the time where you run around your home getting everything ready for your next long day, which is tomorrow. Don't battle too much with it; you know what needs to be done. Instead, don't try to make it as fast as possible, be present and experience the actual motions. Focus on the task at hand and don't think about the next task and the one after that. Leave yourself with enough time to not have to

rush through the things you need to do. Again, any thoughts and anxieties that may come up this time, you may simply acknowledge them and let them pass.

Body Scan Meditation

The second type of meditation we will discuss is commonly known as the Body Scan or Progressive relaxation meditation. We talked about the Body Scan method briefly in our tutorial on mindfulness meditation. In more detail, the body scan practice is a technique that you can perform multiple times a day to help you identify what you are feeling physically and mentally and where you are feeling it as well. Using this technique, you can learn to release the stress carried in your body and mind. Often, when you are stressed, it's very common for it to be held in different areas of your body in the form of tense shoulders, stomach pains, or in many other ways. A lot of the time, you aren't even aware of the stress that you are carrying in your body! When you are really stressed, you may be feeling a lot of physical discomfort but not necessarily connect it with your emotions. The body scan meditation method is effective in relieving stress not only from the mental aspect but in the physical aspect as well. Many research points to the conclusion that there are numerous physical and psychological benefits to relieving tension and relaxing your body.

Relieving physical tension has been proven to decrease psychological stress even when you aren't using any external stress relief efforts. Relieving tension in your body can likely lead to overall lower levels of stress, which then, as a result, leads to less physical tension. This meditation works to break the vicious cycle of mental and physical tension that can feed on itself. Due to this, the body scan meditation is a very effective and useful meditation technique that can help you stay physically and mentally relaxed. It can help you return to a calm state when you notice that you've become too tense. Here is a guide on how you can try the body scan meditation.

1. Find a comfortable place where you can sit down and fully relax your body. It's easier if you are lying down but sitting down is effective as well. Try to find a place and position that is comfortable for you to fully relax but not so comfortable that you may fall asleep easily. Bring your awareness to your breath. Let it slow down and start breathing from deep within your belly instead of your chest. Let your abdomen expand, and then contract with each breath taken. If you find your shoulders moving with each breath, bring your attention to your belly and try breathing from there. Pretend as if it's a balloon

inflating and deflating your abdomen every time you take a breath.

2. This is where we begin to do the actual 'body scan.' Pretend there is a scanner above you or in front of you (if you are sitting down). Imagine that it expels a horizontal laser beam and is slowly scanning your body starting from the top of your head. Bring your awareness to where that scanner is and slowly move it down your body. Do you notice any tension that you feel as you move the scanner through your body? Do you feel any tightness on your shoulders, neck, back, or stomach? Do you feel any sensations of pain, whether it's subtle or sharp? Are you feeling any areas of concentrated energy in your body? If you notice and feel something that is off, try to acknowledge it and think about why it might be. If there is tension, release it and move on. Continue to scan your body all the way down, from your scalp to your ears, to your cheeks, to your chin, to your neck, to your shoulders, and so forth. This becomes more automatic and much easier with practice to the point that you will be able

to do this very quickly and with less effort.

3. Make sure you're bringing attention to areas that you've discovered that have uncomfortable sensations. Breathe into them and watch what happens. Try to imagine the tension leaving your body through the exhale of your breath. A lot of people notice that the feeling of tenseness becomes more intense at first, but continuing to meditate through it allows it to dissipate. Keep your awareness focused on that feeling for a few moments; make sure you are staying present. Feel free to give yourself a light massage in that area if it helps, and move on to the next body part when you're ready.

4. Continue to do this scan with each area of your body, moving from your head to your toes. Make a note of how you feel and which body parts are holding stress. Helping release tension in your body now will allow you to be more aware of it in the future so you can release it as you feel those sensations.

Try to practice the body scan meditation several times throughout the day or during times where you feel stressed. If you are short on time, you can do an abbreviated version of this meditation by sitting down and bringing awareness to any place in your body where you feel that you are carrying tension.

Zen Meditation

Zen meditation is a meditation practice that comes from the Tang Dynasty in ancient China. It is a Buddhist form of meditation. It originates from China, but this popular type of meditation has expanded to Japan and Korea, and many more countries within Asia. There, it thrives to this day.

The term "Zen" is a Japanese word that comes from the Word "Ch'an" in Chinese. It is also a translated form of the term "dhyana," from India, which means meditation or concentration.

This type of meditation is very old, and as I mentioned, it is one of the Buddhist disciplines. Zen Meditation is practiced by both beginners and experienced meditators. One main benefit of this discipline is how it can provide insight into the way that a person's mind functions. This method also provides tools for people who are suffering from depression or anxiety-related problems. However, the main goal of Zen meditation is spiritual. It is meant to uncover the mind's clarity and demonstrate its flexibility.

Different from the basic forms of meditation, Zen meditation helps a person examine deep-seated problems and struggles, and questions of life that have complex answers. Zen meditation delves deeper than other meditation techniques that are focused on relaxing and relieving stress.

Zen meditation is described as "A special transmission outside the teachings; not established upon words and letters; directly pointing to the human heart-mind; seeing nature and becoming a Buddha" by the famous Buddhist master Bodhidharma.

Zen meditation is often learned and practiced in schools of Zen. They normally perform a sitting meditation that is called "zazen." It begins with sitting upright and following the breath, with an emphasis on the movement within the belly. Traditionally, this practice requires a deep and strong connection between the teacher and the pupil. In this case, it would be a dedicated student of Zen and a Zen master.

Zen meditation aims to address core issues rather than creating or providing temporary resolutions for day-to-day life challenges. It explores the deeper causes of unhappiness and turmoil and redirects one's focus as a means of bringing about a deep understanding. In this theory, the key to finding lasting happiness and well-being isn't money or status. In fact, the key lies within all of us. Like other types of spirituality, Buddhism believes that generosity and giving leads to deeper emotional gain. It challenges us to notice and recognize the connection and appreciation that life gives us, and that it is all found within the present moment at any given time.

A Zen master will likely tell you that when you look for inner peace, it will escape you. However, by simply letting go of that idea and by refraining from searching for a reward, you should instead focus on other people's happiness, which will, in turn, provide you with lasting peace.

Although you need to train with a Zen master to understand the complicated depths of this spirituality, I am still able to discuss a few Zen meditation techniques with you. The first is something we recently learned about, which is the observation of the breath. The second technique is quiet awareness. Here the meditator will learn to let their thoughts enter and leave the mind without judging, clinging, or rejecting them. This is similar to the example of watching your thoughts as clouds just pass by you. There is no particular goal to this technique but to just allow their mind to be.

The third technique that Zen meditators use is something called "intensive group meditation." This is a practice that experienced meditators practice most often in temples or meditation centers. During this period, the meditators must spend most of their days in a sitting meditation. They perform this meditation in sessions lasting about 30 - 50 mins in length. Further, they eat all meals in silence during the practice.

Follow-Along Meditation Transcripts

In this subchapter, we will be spending time doing a hands-on practice of meditations. I will provide you with a few guided meditation transcripts. Don't rush into anything; this guide will act as a mere outline for your meditation journey. You can take as much time as you need to get comfortable in a new process. Remember, the transcripts provided here aren't the only transcripts you are allowed to follow; there are hundreds and thousands of different transcripts out there. Don't be afraid to do your own research and find new transcripts to help you with other problems in your life. The most important part of all of this is sticking with meditation every single day. Meditation is only helpful to you when it is fully incorporated into your life.

Positive and Blissful Mind Meditation

You can use this meditation for a time of stress and anxiety. It will help guide you into a more relaxed state where you can focus on the present and find inner peace. Please use this meditation method when you find your mind racing. This can also be used if you feel like you are about to have an anxiety or panic attack.

"Welcome to the positive and blissful mind-guided meditation.

Please find yourself in a quiet area to sit and dim the lighting.

Make sure you are comfortable. Sit with your back straight and shoulders relaxed. Loosen any tight clothing that may be restricting you.

Let your hands lie loosely and relaxed into your lap. Close your eyes and take a deep breath. Now, relax.

Now that your eyes are closed, you may begin to connect with your inner self of thoughts and feelings.

Gradually, let the outside world fade from your awareness.

For the next few minutes, allow yourself to enjoy and submerge into this relaxing experience.

You are free from all your responsibilities during this meditation. Any thoughts, tasks, or concerns that you may have do not require your immediate attention. Tuck those thoughts away and focus on your inner thoughts.

You may find that your mind will begin to wander during this meditation. This is okay, and this is normal. Simply bring your awareness back to the present and to the sound of my voice. I will guide you into a place of inner peace and deep relaxation.

Remember that you are always in control of yourself. If you wish to end this meditation, you can do so by opening your eyes.

Begin to take a slow, long, and deep breath in through your nose. Release that breath through your mouth.

Find your inner self begin to relax.

Begin to take another deep breath in and exhale.
Notice how calming this type of breathing is.
Be aware of the feelings of relaxation starting to spread throughout your body. Starting from your lungs all the way down to your toes.

Continue to breathe deeply, slowly, and gently. Try not to breathe too quickly.

With each inhalation and exhalation, your thoughts start to become lighter.

You may start to feel a sense of spaciousness inside of you. It will open up slowly.

Keep relaxing.

Allow the soft movement of your breath to guide you into an even more relaxed state of being.

Breathe in. Breathe out. Deeper you go into this state of relaxation.

Breathe in. Breathe out. Let your mind gradually slow down. Breathe in. Breathe out. Let it slow down some more.

Breathe in. Breathe out.

You are now in a state of relaxation. You may now begin to enjoy a guided journey into your inner place of joy and serenity.
Allow images and visualizations to form in your mind naturally, as I speak. Do so at your own pace.

If visualizations and mental pictures aren't coming easily to you, simply sense your imaginary surroundings instead of visualizing them.

Begin to let your expectations drift away from you. Let them go. Allow yourself to experience this meditation journey in whatever form comes naturally to you.

Begin to imagine that you are standing in a green and beautiful grassy field. The field stretches on for miles. You can feel the heat of the sun on your face, slowly warming your body.

You feel the soft and lush green grass cushioning your bare feet. You can smell nature all around you.

You can hear the sounds of nature around you. You hear the rustling of the blowing grass. The sounds of birds singing. The rustling of leaves in the distance.

You feel very much at home in this serene place.

You have all the time in the world.

You are safe and happy here.

Take a moment to appreciate your surroundings.

You notice a large luscious tree growing close by.

You begin to walk towards that tree.

Take your time walking. There is no rush whatsoever. Stay in the moment and appreciate the feeling of each step.

As you walk towards the tree, you feel yourself falling more deeply into a state of relaxation.

You are now standing under the tree. Its long branches and large leaves hang right above your head.

You notice that the tree holds many delicious fruits in all shapes, sizes, and colors.

This is not just an ordinary tree. Its fruits carry special powers.

Reach your arm up and take a piece of fruit from the branches. Watch it for a moment. Notice the color of this fruit, the texture, and the weight. It's quite heavy in your hand.

Take a bite of this fruit.

As you swallow the fruit, it slides down your throat and into your belly. You begin to feel something wonderful happen.

A feeling of happiness and peace begins to glow inside of your body.

The sensation starts in your abdomen, and it spreads to your chest and into your heart.

Let go of thinking, and begin to bring all your attention to the feeling. Embellish in the sensation of joy, love, and peace. Feel your body gently glowing with these feelings.

Take another bite of the magical fruit. Taste it. Savor every bite.

This wonderful feeling begins to intensify even more.

Feel yourself begin to radiate this beautiful sensation of love and happiness.

Take another bite of the fruit. Take as many bites as you'd like.

Relax and let yourself drown in this enchanting feeling. Instead of trying, just let it effortlessly take over. Break down any walls that you feel comfortable breaking and let them surround you as much as you like.

Stay with these joyful and peaceful feelings. Enjoy this time of meditation.

You may remain in this relaxed state of meditation for as long as you please. Don't feel rushed to leave."

When you are ready, you may finish this meditation. Simply open your eyes to leave. Take a deep breath and give yourself a few moments to adjust before standing up.

Gratitude Meditation

The Gratitude Meditation is used as a conscious effort to appreciate all the things in the world that makes us feel good. It is directly related to opening our hearts and embracing all our blessings. This meditation is very popular amongst Buddhist monks and nuns. It's typically practiced at the beginning and end of their days to pay gratitude to everything that helped them throughout that day; this also includes their sufferings. Gratitude meditation gives us the power we need to face our problems and weaknesses to acknowledge the darker parts of life. This meditation can be used when you are feeling the burdens of the world. Try this guided meditation when you feel self-pity or hopeless.

Before you begin this meditation, think about something in your life that you are grateful for. Think about where that feeling is held in your body. You can feel grateful for your home, spouse, or even the vacation you just purchased.

"Welcome to the Gratitude Meditation.

Find a comfortable sitting position and dim the lighting.

I will begin by bringing your awareness to the things you are grateful for in life.

Give the sense of gratitude the chance to come up in a natural way. When it arises, let yourself sink into that feeling. Surrender yourself to it. Begin to notice how it feels inside your body, how that energy feels. If the feeling of gratitude does not come up immediately, don't try to force yourself. It is okay. Instead, just surrender yourself to your heart and not your head.

Let's begin to travel through the aspects of your life that you are thankful for. Bring your awareness back to your breath. As you breathe in and breathe out, begin to think about how each breath gives you life.

Bring your awareness to your heart now. Feel it beating, pulsing, filling your body with everything it needs. Feel it being filled with love, joy, and compassion. Feel the peace. Let all these feelings flow through you with each pump.

Now bring your awareness to your ears. Hear the joyous sounds of music, laughter, silence, and the voices of the people you love. Take in the beautiful sounds of life.

Bring your awareness to your face and then to your nose. Remember the smells of the ocean, freshly cut grass, the aroma of freshly baked bread, flowers, nature, the smells that come from the kitchen, and pastries in the oven. Slowly bring your awareness to your lips. Allow it to travel into your mouth. Remember the delicious tastes of food and drinks. The feeling of kisses and laughter. Thank your lips for all the laughter and singing it has produced.

Direct your awareness to your hands. Thank it for everything it has done for you. Allow yourself to feel the feelings of touch, caress, applaud, and squeezing. These are the arms and shoulders that you have used to hug and hold.

Bring your awareness now down to your feet. Wiggle your toes. Your feet have served you well. They transported you, allowed you to walk, run, dance, kick, and leap. Be thankful for them.

Now bring your awareness to your inner self. Your sorrows, tears, and strength that you muster every day to make it through. Thank your inner self for always being there.

Direct your awareness to your growth. Be aware of how you have grown and how your perspective has changed. Be grateful for your ability to see growth and potential in life and other people. Acknowledge your empathy and understanding.

Now, just focus on breathing. Breathe in. Breathe out. Let it be graceful.

Start to experience the warmth, compassion, love, and peace that gratitude brings into your body and into your heart. Savor that feeling. Remember it. Remember that it is always there inside of you. You just have to summon it.

Direct your awareness to the relationships in your life. They have nurtured you at some point in your life. Acknowledge the new ones and the old ones.

Thank all the material things that you have had in your life. Whether they came expectedly or unexpectedly, be grateful for the things you have achieved with commitment and hard work.

Begin to think of love in your life. Think about how the connection feels to those things that are just right.

Remind yourself that when we don't take life for granted, we become thankful for everything that we have.

Breathe in. Breathe out. Let that feeling flow through your body again.

When you are ready to end this meditation, simply just open your eyes.

Stretch your back and shoulders. Take one last deep breath, and carry on about your day."

Spiritual Meditation

This meditation is used for those who want to explore spirituality further. You may not feel any different during this meditation, but you will feel the physical and mental benefits of this practice. During this meditation, you will have to be awake. This technique can lead to sleep. Avoid that to experience spiritual effects.

Before we begin this meditation, think about your own spirituality. What gives you meaning in life? You will need to come up with a word or a short phrase that gives you meaning. You will repeat those words during the time it takes to exhale a breath. For example, if nature holds deep and strong meaning for you, you may select phrases that relate to it.

"Welcome to Spiritual Meditation.

Find a comfortable position for you, one that allows you to remain awake.

Let's begin.

Close your eyes. You can choose to focus your gaze on a small area. Start by relaxing your muscles and relieving any tension you feel.

When you feel thoughts come to your mind, simply acknowledge them and let them pass. Bring your attention back to your body.

Bring your awareness to your breathing. Notice the way each breath feels. Don't try to change your breathing; let it be natural. Just observe.

As thoughts arise in your mind, acknowledge them and let them go. Return your attention to breathing.

Breathe slowly, deeply, and naturally.

If you find your thoughts wandering some more, bring your attention to breathing.

Notice how your breath flows gently in and out through your body. It feels effortless.

Interruptions are normal. You may find yourself thinking about other thoughts. Let them go, and focus on breathing.

Now, begin to think about the meaningful words or phrases you've selected. Begin to say this word in your mind as you breathe out.

Each time you exhale, say the phrase again.

Continue repeating the phrase every time you breathe out.

With each breath, allow distracting thoughts to float by your awareness.

Let any spiritual feeling linger in your body. Don't ignore it, but let it brew deeply inside you. Let it consume your body and let it stay.

Repeat the phrase. Feel the spirituality within you intensify. You may leave this meditation at any moment; simply open your eyes.

Let your body communicate and get comfortable with the feeling of spirituality. Be aware of how it makes you feel.

Begin to bring your awareness back to your breathing. Breathe in. Breathe out. Let your thoughts turn to your body. Relaxed, peaceful, and calm. Notice how your body feels as it becomes more aware of your surroundings.

Bring your attention back to your thoughts. Bring it back to your regular conscious awareness. You may let the spirituality leave your body.

Stay seated for a few more moments with your eyes open. Enjoy the feeling of reawakening. Savor the relaxation and all the other feelings you've encountered.

Begin to reflect on the experience of spiritual meditation. Be aware of all the feelings during the practice. You should be feeling free from worries.

End this guided meditation by wiggling your toes and then your fingers. Stretch your back and shoulders. When you are ready, you may stand up and continue on with your day."

Chapter 3: The Benefits of Meditation

With your new understanding of meditation and mindfulness, we will begin learning about the benefits that meditation will bring into your life. This is a crucial chapter, as practicing meditation without truly understanding its benefits will only increase your chances of giving up before you get to reap the fruits of your labor. Understanding all the benefits that meditation will bring into your day to day life will keep you motivated throughout this important journey. The benefits of meditation begin with improving your mental health, which bleeds into improving your physical health too. This chapter will focus on the most common benefits that people achieve through practicing meditation.

Some people have found that meditation brings about numerous benefits immediately, whereas others have found that it has taken more practice and time to achieve those benefits. Meditation affects you by strengthening your mind and allowing you to be able to control and judge all your thoughts that go through it. Having a strong mind and awareness is said to help achieve your inner peace. Meditation every day is like a workout for your brain. Think of it as something physical, like looking to gain 10 pounds of muscle in the gym. The first few sessions of your workout definitely won't be able to produce anything noticeable. However, you do feel the changes and effects of a workout almost immediately. The more you work out, the stronger and bigger your muscles get. This is exactly like meditation. The first few times you begin to meditate, you may not notice any changes to your stress levels or anxiety levels. However, you will feel the immediate effects of it, which is a sense of relaxation, no matter how little or strong.

The more persistent you are with meditating, you will begin to notice the long-term effects. Due to an increase in mindfulness, you may find yourself having the ability to catch yourself when you begin to daydream or become anxious about something. You will be able to catch yourself in the act of these bad habits and bring your mind back to the present. In addition to that, because meditation brings your awareness to your present surroundings, you will begin to notice little details in life that you may have overlooked in the past. You may start to notice the details of your house plant, or the shape of the clouds, or even notice new details of your own body. Little things like this in life tend to bring us bubbles of joy throughout the day. Allow yourself to savor these moments. Throughout your journey of meditation, I hope that you will begin to achieve more tangible benefits such as; stress reduction, increased emotional health, and sleep improvement.

Stress Relief

Stress is the most common ailment that causes people to pursue meditation. A recent study of 3,500 adults showed that meditation did, in fact, live up to its reputation for reducing stress. Stress, whether it be mental or physical, is caused by increased levels of *cortisol*, which is the body's hormone that is released in response to stress.

This hormone is what causes all the negative symptoms associated with stress. These symptoms include;

- Sleep disruption
- Depression and anxiety
- High blood pressure
- Stress can also lead to tiredness and foggy thinking.

Meditation helps battle stress effectively because being mindful is stress' kryptonite.

Naturally, when humans are in a state of stress, our minds start to go crazy. We begin thinking of all the worst-case scenarios and how that would lead to our untimely demise.

Let's use Heather as an example. Heather works in a lawyers' office as a paralegal and is constantly under a lot of stress. She forgot to submit a document to her boss, which had a deadline of three hours ago. Naturally, Heather's mind goes wild - "My boss is going to be so angry! They are going to sit me down and fire me. I just signed a lease to my new apartment; I can't afford to lose this job! I'm going to have to sell my car and move back in with my parents after this! But I hate living with my parents - they are going to drive me insane. I'll become so depressed and etc. etc. etc." This is where mindfulness comes into play. Instead of spiraling at the thought of the mistake, she made at work; she is able to focus on the task at hand. She would be able to reason with herself and think, "Why am I so scared and stressed?" and be able to answer her own thoughts. Being able to be reasonable with your own thoughts actually prevents spiraling, which in turn reduces stress. With mindfulness, Heather can now say to herself, "Well, I've done a great job in the last year at this job - I don't think my boss will fire me over one missed document. I better go tell them now and submit the document that I've missed." This is the reasonable response that we all want to have in our heads whenever something goes wrong in our lives. Meditation and the practice of mindfulness will be able to help you reduce your anxiety levels.

Pain Management

Over the years, research has found that meditation can improve a person's pain management. Did you know that pain is caused by your mind and not the physical ailments? Your perception of the feeling we call pain is connected to a person's mental state, and can be emphasized and exaggerated during stressful situations.

A study that focused on the relationship or pain and mindfulness used MRI techniques to observe brain activity while participants felt a painful stimulus. One group of participants had gone through four days of meditation and mindfulness training, while the other group had not. The patients who went through the meditation training had increases in brain activity in the areas that control pain. Further, they reported a lower sensitivity to the pain stimuli.

An even bigger experiment examined the effects of regular meditation in 3,500 people. Its results showed that meditators were associated with lower companies of intermittent or chronic pain. Another study on people who had terminal illnesses showed that meditation and mindfulness helped manage and mitigate chronic pain near the end of their life. In all of the above scenarios, meditators and non-meditators all experienced the exact same causes of pain, but those who meditated showed a greater ability to cope with pain and even experienced a smaller sensation of pain. Overall, the many studies conducted lead to the conclusion that meditation can help diminish pain perception, and this may be used to help treat chronic pain when used for medical care or physical therapy. If you are someone that is suffering from chronic pain, meditation may be a great way for you to manage it better without the need for prescription drugs.

Improving Sleep

One of the most noted benefits is that meditation helps improve sleep quality and prevents insomnia. Nearly half the population in the world has struggled with insomnia at some point in their life. Meditation and mindfulness help you acknowledge and let thoughts pass through your mind allowing you to clear it of any lingering thoughts. Being able to acknowledge thoughts and let them go plays a huge part in one's ability to fall asleep. If you have many things on your mind, it tends to lead to the inability to fall asleep. It creates stress and anxiety, which is a good night's sleep's worst enemy.

A scientific experiment looked at two meditation and mindfulness programs and compared them by randomly putting the participants into one of the two groups. The first practiced meditation and the second group did not. The first group was able to fall asleep quicker and remain in a sleeping state for longer than the second group. Thus, regularly practicing meditation and mindfulness helps one control and redirect the "runaway" or "leftover" thoughts in one's head, which often leads to insomnia. In addition, meditation helps you to relax the body, which releases tense muscles and can place you into a calmer state where you will be more likely to fall asleep.

Addiction Management

Recently, studies have found that meditation can help fight addictions. This benefit is one of the more unheard of ones as it helps a very niche market. Meditation, the simplest terms, is just mental discipline. You can think of it as mental weight lifting. The mental discipline you build through meditation helps you break dependencies by increasing self-control and awareness of triggers with addictive behaviors. Research has proven that meditation can help people increase their understanding of the causes behind their addictive behaviors and help them find techniques to redirect attention, as well as improve self-control and willpower, and also to control their impulses and emotions.

An experiment took alcoholics and made meditation a part of their routines, and it was discovered that meditation helped them to better control their cravings and lower stress associated with it. This training can additionally help people control their cravings associated with food consumption. Fourteen other experiments found that meditation aided people in controlling binge eating and emotional eating. If you are currently facing any addiction problems yourself, consider practicing meditation to help you understand your own behaviors and learn to start changing them.

Improving Emotional Health

Meditation has been proven to help with a person's emotional health and mental health. Stress and anxiety are partners in crime, just like how your emotional health and the overall state of your mind have a close relationship. Lowering negative emotions such as stress and anxiety leaves room in your mind for more positive emotions such as happiness and calmness. There are forms of meditation out there that can help a person lead to a better self-image and build a more positive outlook on life. In the same study discussed above, those who meditated experienced long term decreases in depression and better overall emotional health. A few other scientific studies suggest that meditation can treat depression by decreasing cytokines. Cytokines are inflammatory chemicals in your brain that are released in response to stress, which negatively affects a person's mood and can lead to depression in the long run.

Increasing Self-Awareness

Practicing meditation enhances one's self-awareness. Since meditation helps you increase mindfulness, it will also naturally increase your self-awareness as you're paying more attention to your thoughts. Self-awareness allows you to develop a stronger understanding of yourself and why you think the things you do, which helps you grow into the best version of yourself. This benefit particularly helps people who face social anxiety problems. Being mindful of your actions, facial expressions, tone of voice, and other forms of body language is a great way to know if you're acting in a socially acceptable manner. Having good self-awareness is beneficial as society treats people who have it better than those who don't. It allows you to understand oneself more and, in return, have the ability to understand other people more. Being self-aware actually creates compassion and sympathy, not only for others - but for yourself as well.

Increasing Attention Span

Meditation has also been known to help improve a person's attention span. Have you ever noticed that you are unable to focus on something for an extended amount of time? A common example would be starting to watch a new television show. You may find yourself drifting off after the first two minutes of a new show and end up doing something out of bad habit like scrolling on your phone with the TV playing in the background. This is all due to having a short attention span. There is a type of meditation called 'focused-attention' meditation that is specifically used to combat this problem. This type of meditation is like making your attention span practice weight lifting to become stronger. Its goal is to help increase the endurance and strength of your attention. A recent study looked into the effects of an 8-week meditation and mindfulness course. It found that practicing this specific type of meditation improved their attention span, as well as their ability to shift attention from one task to another.

A related study that focused on human resource workers showed that the people who were trained in mindfulness and did it regularly were able to stay focused on one task for a longer period of time. In addition, these works also were able to remember the details of their assignment, whereas the people who did not meditate, did not. Another review showed meditation to help reverse bad habits within the brain that are associated with worrying and daydreaming. Overall, meditating for short periods of time can improve someone's attention span. Another study showed that even 3-5 days of meditation practice could improve your attention span.

Improving Memory

Research has also found that meditation helps reduce age-related memory loss. Scientifically, people who don't actively use their brains tend to have them deteriorate faster. This is why in a lot of senior homes, nurses and workers promote brain games for the seniors to prevent deterioration. Games that stimulate your brain, like chess, mahjong, and even video games, help exercise your brain's functions to keep it healthy. "Kirtan Kriya" is a meditation form that incorporates a chant and a repetitive finger motion to help focus your thoughts. It is said to help improve a person's performance in memory-related tests in a variety of studies that looked at memory loss due to age.

One review of 10 further experiments found several other meditation styles to also increase a person's memory, attention span, and mental speediness in senior subjects.

To summarize, not only can meditation fight standard memory loss related to age, but it can also help improve memory in people that are battling dementia. Suppose there is a history of Alzheimer's or dementia in your family. In that case, meditation may be something you'd want to incorporate into your life, so slow down the effects of these diseases.

Generating More Kindness

One of the more known benefits of meditation is that it helps generate kindness. There are specific types of meditation that actually focus more on increasing positive actions and feelings towards others and yourself. Metta is a type of meditation that is more commonly known as the loving-kindness meditation. Its entire theory rests on developing compassionate thoughts and feelings toward yourself. With practice, people learn to show kindness and forgiveness externally - usually to friends, then acquaintances, and lastly, enemies. It is actually proven to be easier to extend compassion and kindness externally than internally. By mastering kindness externally, it helps one give more compassion and kindness to themselves. When you show yourself more kindness and compassion, you can reduce negative symptoms like anxiety, depression, and insomnia. One study of 100 adults assigned at random to a program that practiced loving-kindness meditation found that its benefits were dependent on dosage. In other words, the more time and effort that the people put into Metta meditation, the more positive feelings of kindness they experienced. Another similar study showed that people's positive feelings after practicing Metta meditation could improve anger management, marital conflict, and overall social anxiety. Based on this research, meditation benefits seem to build up and grow over time as long as Metta meditation is regularly practiced.

Chapter 4: Meditation Mantras

In this chapter, we are going to look at meditation mantras and affirmations, which can help you greatly in achieving your goals because of the positive mental state that they will put you in. This will also help you increase your overall self-esteem and mental state.

What Is a Mantra?

Having a mantra may seem a little airy-fairy if you are not usually one to use this type of thing, but it proves quite helpful in times of intense emotion. A mantra is a word or a phrase that you repeat which is designed to help you concentrate on meditation. In day to day life, though, it helps bring your consciousness back to the moment, just like meditation does. Your mantra can be anything, such as "relax," "you're safe," or anything that helps you to calm yourself at the moment. Decide on your mantra in a calm and quiet moment so that it is ready in the back of your mind when you need it in a moment of anger.

Affirmations are very similar to mantras. By definition, they are something that is spoken or written, which states something to be true. More specifically, affirmations are the valuable and uplifting assurances that we tell ourselves. They are words or phrases that we use to state something about ourselves or our lives to be true. Another similar term would be declarations. The difference between affirmations and declarations is that declarations can be an opinion or a belief rather than a fact. The word declaration can be used as a noun or as a verb, as in *to make a declaration*, which is when you share your declaration with others in the form of writing or speaking.

We will look at some examples of mantras, affirmations, and declarations below, and I will teach you how to make some for yourself in order to use them in your own life. Please note that we can use the terms mantra, affirmation, and declaration interchangeably from here forward.

Benefits of Having a Mantra

Mantras can be used as a type of affirmation or a tool when doing a specific type of meditation.

Having a mantra ready to go can help you focus on the meditation you are doing. Like I mentioned above, mantras can also be used in a state of high emotion. When you have a mantra in mind and ready to go, you may be able to use it at a moment's notice.

How to Use a Mantra/Affirmation

The technique of implementing change that lasts is to change the way someone perceives themselves. So how does a mantra or affirmation play a role here? Affirmations are very effective when used out loud so that you are able to hear the positive reminders being said in your own voice. Humans naturally believe the things that they tell themselves. For example, if someone dislikes some aspect of their physical appearance, they will believe that they are unattractive. The next time you are in front of a mirror, practice using affirmations by saying something you like about yourself. By repeating this every time, you are in front of a mirror will eventually lead you to believe these positive things, and you will begin to focus on the positive rather than what you don't like about yourself.

If someone is trying to improve their self-esteem or their negative mind state, the affirmations they use should be focused solely on positive things. Suppose a person wishes to use affirmations in order to achieve specific goals. In that case, it is beneficial for them to use affirmations that remind them of their positive personal values and their potential. Frequently repeating your affirmations aloud to yourself, or even writing them down (or better yet, a combination of both), will aid you in building a positive self-narrative. This positive narrative will lead to an increase in your level of self-esteem over time, and thus, a greater likelihood of achieving your goals.

We will look at the steps you will need to take to create your own affirmations below, and once you have created them for yourself, you will be ready to begin using them right away. Once you have completed your positive affirmations, schedule a block of time every day or a couple of times per week to take a look back at them and update them. The more you read them and drill them into your memory, the more positive thoughts will naturally come to you. You can also document any changes you feel in yourself as you do this exercise.

How to Make Your Own Mantra or Affirmation

1. Structure your mantra/affirmation

To begin, you want to structure your mantra/affirmation so that it begins with something called an *"I statement*." This means that you want to start your sentence with *"I am..."*

2. Focus on creating mantras/affirmations that have a positive outcome.

Try to refrain from using avoidant words such as "not" in your statements. Make them as positive as you can, as your brain feels positive when it hears positive words like "can!"

3. Keep your mantras/affirmations as concise as you can.

Ensure they are concise so that they guide you to the point and serve as quick reminders of positivity.

4. Design your mantras/affirmations to be as specific as possible.

This is especially important if it guides you to your goal, as you want to ensure that you are keeping yourself focused on the goal so that you are continuously reminding yourself of it.

5. Try to write your mantras/affirmations in the present tense.

Focus on using a word that ends with "ing"; this will help you ensure that you are using the word's present tense.

6. Use descriptive words.

Using descriptive words will give your affirmation more impact and will make it more detailed.

7. Make your affirmations personal to you and your situation.

Ensure that your affirmations relate to your specific goals or whatever you are dealing with at the moment; this will increase their impact when you use them and help you remember why you are using them.

Part 2

Chapter 5: Breathing for Meditation

A major component of meditation is breath awareness. Not only is it a technique that is used in many types of meditation, but it can also be an entire meditation on its own. Breath awareness meditation helps combat anxieties and stress that can be caused by our bodies not breathing properly. When people are under a lot of stress and anxiety, it is natural to hold their breath. Have you ever noticed that you haven't breathed in a while when you are in a stressful situation? We will learn more about how to combat unhealthy breathing habits, leading to a decline in physical and psychological health. This type of meditation is thoroughly integrated into yoga culture and tradition. It plays a huge role in every aspect of the practice. In fact, this is so important that instructors claim that yoga is not yoga without breath awareness. The practice of breath awareness did come from the Buddhists and early Christian teachers as well. This section will learn the technique of breath awareness in meditation and how it's also used in yoga.

How to Practice Proper Breathing Techniques During Meditation

Below are a series of steps that will help you master your breathing techniques during meditation. Please follow along and try to practice this in every meditation that you do.

1. Begin by sitting in a comfortable place with your back straight on a chair, bench, or even a cushion. Close your eyes and rest your body for a few moments. Try to soften the sides of your rib cage along with your abdominal wall. This will allow your breath to flow deeper. You will begin to notice a cleansing sensation when you exhale and a feeling of nourishment when you inhale. BE patient, and allow the relaxed movement of your inhale and exhale to become smooth. It will likely take several minutes for you to sense that it is quite effortless. When you have achieved this, you are ready to continue to the next step.

2. Next, relax your body, beginning from your head all the way down to your toes. Feel the sensation of relaxation from your toes back to your head. Start to slowly move your attention through the body, releasing tensions just like the body scan technique. When you are finished, return to the top of your head and sense your entire body as a whole. Breathe as if your whole body is taking a breath. Let yourself follow the effortlessness of your breath. As time goes by, continue to observe your breath.

3. Bring your awareness to the touch of the air in the nostrils. Start to transition from breathing with your whole body to breathe in with your nostrils. Allow it to feel natural and comfortable, and give yourself a few minutes to do this. Bring your attention back to your breathing if your mind starts to wander off. Throughout your practice sessions, train yourself to maintain your focus and try not to break your awareness or breathing. Your mind won't stop thinking, so don't expect it to. Instead, just maintain breath awareness.

4. When thoughts arise in your mind, let them come and go. Do not focus your attention and awareness on them but do not turn them into your enemy either. Just simply let it go by you like a cloud. As you continue through this exercise, your breath awareness will deepen. IT will slowly become deeply relaxing, and you will begin to notice changes in the state of your awareness. These subtle changes are important checkpoints to your concentration and signal that your breath awareness meditation has nearly completed its inner work.

Breath Awareness Meditation in Yoga

1. In yoga, two reclining postures are used to simplify the early stages of breath training. Savasana, which is the corpse pose, is done in a supine posture. Makarasana is the crocodile pose that is done by lying on the stomach. The supine pose is used to observe the relaxed abdominal breathing, while the crocodile pose is used to observe the deep, diaphragmatic breathing.
2. Be sure to be aware of your breathing, not only during yoga or meditation. Notice it after you climb a long flight of

stairs or while you're swimming underwater. The goal here is to be able to watch your own breathing with a certain detachment. Try to become the student of your own breath.

3. Try to make sure that your yoga breathing is optimal. This requires your breathing to be; diaphragmatic, nasal, deep, smooth, even, without sound, and without pause.

4. Once you master your breathing skills in supine and crocodile pose, you will begin to implement these skills in standing postures as well.

Chapter 6: Tips for Success

Mindfulness and meditation are great ways to reduce your stress levels and get in touch with your body and its sensations. Mindfulness is about bringing your consciousness to the present moment and focusing on your body, its sensations, the sounds it hears, and what it feels like from the inside. Mindfulness involves noticing the thoughts that come into your mind and letting them pass by, not paying them too much attention. Mindfulness is a great practice for those who have difficulty getting out of their heads and tend to think quite a bit. You can use mindfulness for a variety of reasons, but here we will focus on its use for reducing stress and anxiety and getting in touch with your body on a physical level. Mindfulness and meditation go hand in hand. Meditation increases mindfulness while mindfulness improves and deepens meditation. Meditation is a practice, while mindfulness is a state of being.

Getting Into a Mindful State

To get into a state of mindfulness involves getting quiet and observing, without judgment, everything that occurs within your body. You must let your thoughts drift by, noticing but not judging them. Pay attention to sensations in your body. For example, is there tightness or tension anywhere in your body? Be aware of the feelings of your chest rising during every breath and the weight of your body on the chair. Notice also your emotions and feelings. By doing this over and over again, you will be able to eventually focus on your body with less and less distracting thoughts. When your thoughts start to distract you, bring your attention back to your body and your breathing. Being able to reach a state like this allows you to reconnect with your body from the inside and is beneficial for reducing your anxiety and stress levels.

Being able to reach a state like this allows you to reconnect with your body from the inside. Approaching your body with a non-judgment mindset will also make it easier for you to change your beliefs about your body or introduce new thoughts and behaviors. Instead of letting your mind spiral with anxious *what-if* thoughts, you will not let them escalate. They will not escalate to the level they normally would because instead of judging yourself and your body and worrying about what is wrong with you, you will approach it as is and without trying to force anything.

By focusing on the body and letting your thoughts enter your consciousness one by one, you can untangle them, resulting in a reduction in stress level. The state of meditation also brings about a state of relaxation and calm. Many times, we are running around with a mind full of running thoughts, one after the other. When we take time to sit in silence, breathe, and sort through everything we are thinking and feeling through a non-judgmental lens, it leads to a state of inner peace. This state of inner peace makes it much easier for your body to let in and embrace the good feelings and allows your mind to be more open and receptive to them.

The Best Space to Practice Meditation

It may be difficult to find the 'best' space to begin practicing meditation and mindfulness in our busy modern-day lives. In reality, you can practice meditation at any time and especially during the busiest times of your day. You can practice meditation during times where you think you shouldn't, such as during working hours or during your daily commute. Let's learn about how we can practice meditation during these busy times.

Practicing Meditation During Commuting Hours

We can all agree that one of the most dreaded daily activities is the commute to work. In fact, according to many studies, this is so dreaded that a long commute is one of the major stressors in life that decreases happiness. The easy answer in this situation is to just move and live closer to where you work and keep your commute short. However, unless you have tons of money - this may not be feasible for many. So, how do we increase our happiness during the awful chore of the commute? The answer is to practice mindful commuting. By practicing meditation, you have achieved an increased level of mindfulness. Take that one step further and extend that mindfulness not only during meditation time but during your commute as well.

Let's use the example of driving to work. This is the perfect place to practice mindfulness. It helps keep the anger and stress at bay when we encounter situations that induce road rage. Rather than finishing your drive stressed out and upset, you can end your drive feeling refreshed and ready to work. It's extremely easy to tune things out and get lost in your thoughts while driving. For some reason, our autopilot takes over, and you get to the office safely (most of the time). Mindful driving is all about being present during the actual drive. It allows us to move away from obsessive and negative thoughts and gives us a chance to appreciate the world we live in. Here are some tips on how you can practice mindful driving.

1. When you first get into your car, take a few controlled breaths. Acknowledge that you are now in your car and are about to start driving.

2. Turn off your radio and keep your phone on silent. Try to eliminate all potential distractions that could occur in your drive.

3. Take a moment to take in your surroundings and the silence in your car. What color is your dashboard? Do you hear the rumbling of your engine?

4. As you begin to drive, start paying attention to your surroundings. You may begin to notice different things on the route to work that you've never noticed before. Take in the sights, sounds, and scenery of your drive.

5. Focus your attention on the physical experience of driving. Pay attention to where your hands are placed on the steering wheel. What does it feel like sitting in your seat? How do the pedals feel against the sole of your shoe?

6. Begin to shift your focus to other physical sensations in your body. Do you feel the tension in your shoulders or your neck? Do you have a headache? Do your hips feel tight from sitting for long periods? Relax the parts of your body that feel tense, and you will start to feel some of the pain and stress leave your body.

7. Suppose you encounter a stressful situation while driving, such as being cut off. Try to notice the feelings that this brings. Does it bring your frustration? Anger? Anxiety? Maybe even induce some competitiveness? Acknowledge and identify these emotions and understand why you are feeling them. Often, simply understanding why you feel a negative emotion will help you feel less negative.

8. When you stop at a red light or stop sign, take a moment, and do a quick breathing exercise. Take a few deep and calming breaths 3 - 4 times before you start the car again.

9. Any time your mind begins to wander, gently pull your awareness back to the present. An untrained mind naturally

80

jumps from topic to topic quickly. Statistically, the average person thinks as many as 50,000 different thoughts every day. You can't stop it completely during but practicing mindful driving will redirect these monkeying thoughts to focus on the actual act of driving. Remember, when you notice yourself thinking about anything that is not the task at hand - take a deep breath and bring your awareness back.

Practicing Meditation During Working Hours

Let's discuss how meditation and mindfulness at work will benefit our everyday life. We have all had the experience of feeling overwhelmed and scattered at work. This could be caused by too many projects or a sense of demotivation to complete current assignments. Did you know that motivation in the workplace is directly linked to mindfulness? Our ability to stay focused and mindful at work is a way to reprogram our minds to think healthier and less stressful. Below are some benefits to how mindful working can improve your everyday life.

First off, mindfulness in the workplace helps with stress reduction. This is a dominant cause of employee disengagement. The European Agency for Safety and Health at Work conducted a study that produced the statistic that more than half of 550 million working days are lost every year from absenteeism are stress-related. Also, 80% of employees report that they feel stress from their workplace and need help learning how to manage it. Some forward-thinking companies nowadays, such as Google and Adobe, all have formal mindfulness programs incorporated into the workplace to promote stress reduction in employees. However, if you already practice meditation, you don't need to worry if your workplace doesn't offer a program like this. You can do it yourself.

Mindfulness in the workplace also leads to higher absorption of new information. Scientific facts point to allowing your brain to break from developing new skills, critical thinking, and problem-solving to increase learning and creativity. Not taking enough breaks altogether leads to increased tiredness, stress, and thinking blocks. This holds especially true for those who work in jobs that require an extended period of focus.

Adaptability is something that can increase when you are mindful at work. Being able to adapt quickly and efficiently is crucial at work. Interestingly, most employers now value resourcefulness and adaptability over hard skills like coding or programming? Adaptability means that you can quickly adjust accordingly to new situations and handle multiple requests at once. The more you expose yourself to different ways of doing tasks, learning, and gaining confidence in moments of uncertainty, the more adaptable you will become. Adaptability is one of the most important characteristics of excellent leadership performance. It's typically present in leaders who can manage changing priorities and are comfortable in adjusting their perceptions and beliefs.

Problem-solving abilities are enhanced when you are mindfully working. Problem-solving is the ability to remove chaos from the untrained mind. Removing that clutter leads to better concentration, which ultimately leads to untying the complicated knot of problem-solving. Also, mindfulness helps with problem-solving by freeing you from distractions and giving you a new angle to attack from. When you are at the heart of a challenge, try to practice mindfulness. You may be surprised at the increased ability to process information in different ways that are required for a resolution.

Being mindful in the workplace also helps facilitate creativity. The fundamental aspect of creativity is divergent thinking. This refers to the ability to come up with ideas that are outside the box. By practicing mindfulness at work, you may be able to enhance creativity, which allows you to think more innovatively than those who are mindless. Mindfulness helps free your mind from distractions, which in turn boosts your ability to look at things around you from a new perspective.

Vitality in the workplace is also strengthened when you are working mindfully. By definition, vitality means 'exuberant physical strength of mental vigor.' In our case, mindfulness increases a person's vitality, or in other words; their mental vigor. Every single day you go to work with a certain amount of energy. Some days if you've had a healthy sleep, you may have high energy. Some days if you've had a rough night's sleep, you may feel like you're running on an empty gas tank. Vitality is an essential element in accomplishing tasks while being able to enjoy the work you are doing at the same time. Continuing to stay focused and mindful is proven to positively affect your vitality as it helps you remain aware of your goals and dreams. When your aspirations are clear to you, you are more likely to work towards them when you've got high vitality.

When you are working mindfully in the workplace, you'll likely notice that you have increased empathy towards others. We've all heard the saying "to stand in someone else's shoes." Empathy plays a huge role in understanding the minds of other people and relating emotionally with others. Practicing mindfulness at work enables us to have the room in our brain that is used to feel empathy for other people.

The Best Moments of the Day to Meditate

- The best space to practice meditation
- The best moments of the day to meditate
- Notes on posture and positioning

Chapter 7: How to Choose Your Method

Choosing the right meditations for your personal purposes is a huge part of your meditation journey. In this chapter, I will be teaching you how to choose the best method of meditation by trying all the different types you've learned. This process will span over a few days, so be sure to be patient with yourself as you are learning what feels good for you and what doesn't.

Step One (Day One):

- Day one of your meditation journey will mostly consist of planning, goal setting, and creating accountability for yourself. Remember, meditation is meant to help you in the long term, so doing it once a month won't benefit you much. You must achieve to incorporate it into your everyday life.

- Select your meditation of choice; you can have one more than once, but most would recommend practicing a maximum of two, so you can master them more easily. A good way of discovering which type of meditation works best with you is to try them all. This guide will help you try the four most common types of meditation (Mindfulness, body scan, and breath awareness). Make your decision based on your findings. Yoga is also a type of meditation, so you can choose this method if you want it to be a more physical activity.

- Make a plan for when you will meditate. Determine how much time your schedule will allow for at least 15 minutes of meditation a day. As mentioned in the previous chapter, if you are working with a tighter schedule, identify your day's times where you have to do a mindless task like driving or brushing your teeth. These times are also suitable for meditation. My recommendation for beginners, however, is to set aside a time block for meditation.

- Create accountability for yourself so you continue to meditate for the times you told yourself to. This can be as simple as a calendar reminder on your computer or phone. It can also be a family member or a spouse that will hold you accountable for this task. If you have chosen to meditate through yoga, signing up for classes is a good way to hold yourself accountable.

- Invest in something that will help make meditation fun. In my experience, I find lighting incense before I begin my practice to be extremely soothing and helps the overall meditation session.

Step Two (Day Two):

- This is actually your first real day of meditation. As mentioned on day one, it is important to try all types of meditation and select the ones that suit you the best that you will choose to practice moving forward. We will begin by trying mindfulness meditation.

- Find a comfortable place; this is your first time practicing meditation. Let's flip back to the earlier chapters where we discussed how to perform a mindfulness meditation. It is also incredibly beneficial to also listen to an audio meditation guide of the type of meditation you're practicing. In this situation, since we are practicing mindfulness meditation, you can explore resources like YouTube or Podcasts that have guided mindfulness meditation.

- Close your eyes and while in a sitting position, imagine as if your thoughts are clouds and you are lying on your back cloud gazing. With every thought that goes by, simply acknowledge them and let it float away.

- Your mind will likely wander during your first time meditating. That's okay; bring your awareness and your thoughts back to the present. Try to identify what thought led your mind to wander off, and then take a breath and focus again on the clouds passing by, which are your thoughts.

- When you are finished with your first mindfulness meditation, document your findings. Did you drift off a lot? Did you notice any particular thoughts or feelings in your body? How do you feel after the meditation compared to before?

Step Three (Day Three):

- On your third day of meditation, we will try out a different method. Today, we will be trying the body scan meditation. This one is one of the easier meditation techniques as you can literally do it anywhere.

- First, find a comfortable place if you are a beginner. As you remember, in Chapter Two, we discussed how to do a body scan technique. Begin by imagining a scanner above you if you are lying down or in front of you if you are sitting down. Imagine it to have a horizontal laser beam that starts at the top of your head and scans your body down to your toes.

- This beam moves slowly, and every time it passes a body part, it brings your awareness to it. Do you notice any aches, tension, or particular feelings? If you do, acknowledge it and release the tension you feel. If it's an ache, give it a quick massage and move on to the next body part.

- When you are finished with your first body scan meditation, document your findings. Which areas of your body did you notice to be the tensest or have the most pain? Was it your shoulders or stomach? Make a note of this, and you will likely be able to discover where your body tends to hold stress. Make a note of how you feel after this meditation technique compared to before.

Step Four (Day Four):

- On the fourth day of meditation, we will practice the breath awareness meditation technique. This meditation is the backbone of yoga and also a meditation technique in itself. Those who want a more physical experience of meditation should consider practicing meditation through yoga. Breath awareness is a non-negotiable part of yoga.

- We will begin the breath awareness meditation by sitting in a comfortable place with your back straight on a chair. Begin breathing deeply and allow yourself to feel the nourishment of every breath. Again, refer to the more detailed Breath Awareness Meditation guide in Chapter two if you don't remember.

- Make sure that you have relaxed your body from your head down to your toes throughout this meditation. With more practice sessions in the future, you will be able to train yourself to maintain your focus and try not to break awareness or breathing.

- At the end of this meditation, make sure to document moments where your awareness drifted away from your breath. Were you able to bring your awareness back? How long did it take? Have you started to notice any changes in your state of awareness?

Step Five (Day five):

- Day five of meditation, you have already tried the three most common types of meditation practices for beginners. It is time to compare notes of all three and determine which one or two is most suitable for you to pursue. Once you have selected which meditation

practices to pursue, begin to start
practicing your most enjoyable one.

- When you've finished practicing your
  selected technique, make sure to
  document your findings again. How did
  it feel the second time practicing this
  meditation? Was it the same? Harder?
  Easier? How do your mind and body feel
  afterward?

- At this point in our 10-day guide, it is
  also important to assess yourself. Are
  you able to hold yourself accountable? If
  not, are the ways you've set up to hold
  yourself accountable working? Do you
  need to reassess your approach to
  meditation? Make sure you have time in
  your day to give to meditation.

Step Six (Day six):

- Welcome to day six of meditation. You
  have now tried all the meditation
  techniques and have selected one or two
  to focus on for the rest of this guide. On
  this day, you are going to try to
  incorporate meditation into your daily
  routine activities instead of setting aside
  a time block for it.

- Identify when you have an opportunity to meditate while you are doing something else. Ideal activities for this include; brushing your teeth, driving, washing the dishes, and during exercise.

- Make sure that you really pay attention to the sounds and smells around you as a part of this practice. This will help bring you into the moment.

- This type of practice tends to be more difficult when you have more distractions around you. Make sure to document your findings after. How difficult did you find this meditation? Do you feel differently about the activity you were meditating in?

Step Seven (Day Seven):

- On your seventh day of meditation, you should start to feel more confident and more comfortable in your routine. We will take it one step further, and you will try to incorporate Mindful Observation into your day.

- Before you begin the practice of your meditation of choice, we are going to try a mindful observation exercise. Select an

object in your immediate area, ideally
something that is organic, like a plant,
insect, or fruit. Begin to watch the object
as if you were looking at it for the first
time. Don't do anything else except
notice the object you are watching.

- Explore the object visually by focusing
  on its shape and formation. Allow
  yourself to be consumed by its presence.
  Try to connect with its energy and its
  natural purpose in the world. Refer to
  earlier chapters if you need a more
  detailed walkthrough on how to practice
  mindful observation.

- Once you have completed that exercise,
  it is time to practice your meditation of
  choice.

- Try to practice mindful observation
  throughout your day after this
  meditation session. Make a note of
  details in things around you that you've
  never noticed before.

- At the end of day eight, document if you
  feel differently. Do you find meditation
  getting easier or harder? Is your current
  routine working for you? Do you feel like

you have developed good meditation habits?

Step Eight (Day Eight):

- On your eighth day of meditation, you will begin your day with your meditation routine. We are going to take meditation even further by extending it to other areas of your life. As we discussed in Chapter 5, it is important in your meditation journey to accomplish activities like mindful observation, eating, commuting, and working.

- Begin your meditation as you usually would. Make sure you are still maintaining good posture, habits, and technique. Incorporate a mindful observation exercise at the beginning or end of your meditation. Choose a different object this time.

- When you've finished your meditation, keep in mind that you will be practicing mindful eating, commuting, and working throughout the day.

- To practice mindful eating, isolate a 15-minute block for one meal of your day to sit down by yourself to eat. Avoid any distractions that could arise like; other people, televisions, computers, and moving around. Plan to serve your meal on a plate or bowl. If you know you will be purchasing takeout, bring a plate or bowl with you. Make a conscious effort to chew your food properly. Stop eating when you feel about 80% full. If you are feeling stuffed during your meal, you have overeaten. Refer back to Chapter 5 for a more detailed guide on how to perform mindful eating.

- Next, we will practice mindful commuting. Pick a place that you will need to go to that day. This could be to work, to the grocery store, or to the gym. If you are driving, make sure there are minimal distractions. Turn off any music or radio and begin to focus on the act of driving itself. If you are using public transit, avoid listening to music or scrolling on your phone. Pay attention to your environment. Observe the people around you and listen to the noises in your surroundings. You should immediately start to feel differently in this commute.

- Lastly, we will extend your mindfulness to working as well. Pay attention to the work you are doing and try to think outside of the box. Instead of rushing through things, try to think about them more deeply. Try to notice if this is helping with any stress or anxiety that you normally feel while working.

- At the end of the ninth day of meditation, remember to document your findings. What was it like to practice mindfulness all throughout the day? How did you feel about eating mindfully? What things did you notice during your commute when you were mindful? Do you feel more at peace with yourself? Are you enjoying meditation?

Step Nine (Day Nine and Beyond):

- On our last day of meditation, I want us to focus on another day of practicing mindfulness exercises. You have now accomplished a week of having continuous sessions of meditation, trying mindfulness exercises, and documenting your findings. The goal of this day is to incorporate these exercises into your everyday life.

- As usual, begin your day with your regular meditation session. If you have the time, you may add a whole other session just to the mindful observation practice. You may multitask your mindful observation exercise with your mindful commuting exercise if you are tight on time.

- Next, block off another 15 minutes in your day for mindful eating. If possible, challenge yourself to do this at every meal. If you are eating a meal with another person, invite them to try mindful eating with you. This can lead to a good discussion of the food and how it tastes or feels.

- Practice mindful commuting whenever you have to go somewhere. Try to get used to doing this whenever you are driving, walking, or using public transit. If you are walking, you can also practice mindful observation of the nature around you.

- When you are working, try to be mindful of the entirety of it. Multiple studies have proved this to reduce stress. Since most people are working for atlas eight hours of the day, being mindful during all that time can help to achieve inner peace and better mental wellbeing.

- At the end of day ten, do some self-reflection. Think back to the beginning of your meditation journey. What changes do you feel? Do you feel a decreased level of stress, anxiety, and depression? Are you able to practice self-love more easily? Have you begun to notice the beauty of the world around you? Do you feel more at peace with yourself? If you answer yes to atlas one of those questions, it means meditation is already beginning to help you. Grasp onto that success as a milestone, and don't give up.

Chapter 8: Example Mantras

Mantras are often something that you see on television as the stereotypical way to 'meditate.' Although these portrayals of mantras are not 100% accurate, there are many benefits to creating and using one throughout your meditation journey. Using Mantras often sound a little cheesy or awkward, but it is a great coping technique specific to moments of high emotion. Telling yourself a mantra during an intense situation is one good way to center yourself back in the moment. Try repeating simple positive and encouraging phrases like "This is just a temporary feeling." or "I am okay, I will be okay." or "I'm not in danger; I just need to focus on my breathing."

Transcendental Meditation

Transcendental Meditation is a type of meditation that utilizes the power of mantras. This type of meditation is the most unique but also has no reported health benefits. However, it is meant for those who want to expand their spiritual horizons. Transcendental Meditation (TM) refers to a form of silent mantra meditation. Maharishi Mahesh Yogi created this technique and introduced it to India's Transcendental Meditation movement during the 1950s.

This type of meditation practice involves the use of a mantra twice a day for 15 - 20 minutes each time while sitting with your eyes closed. This technique is reportedly the most widely practiced and most widely researched meditation technique. There are hundreds of published research studies based on this. You can only learn this technique from certified TM teachers through a seven-step course. IT's costs vary in different countries. TM was so big back in the 1960s that it was incorporated into many schools, universities, corporations, and prison programs in the United States, Latin America, Europe, and India. This technique is deeply rooted in Hinduism but is described as both religious and non-religious.

Chapter 9: How to Make Meditation a Daily Practice

In the earlier chapters, you learned how to select and use a meditation method of your choice. If you've already done this, then you are in a great position to make meditating a part of your daily practice. This can prove challenging for many people as many bad habits can easily prevent someone from meditating every day. It is crucial that you learn how to develop new habits that allow you to meditate on a daily basis. In this chapter, I will be teaching you about the power of habits and how you can use them to help you meditate every day. Let's start with learning the basics of developing a new habit.

Building New Habits

The first thing I will teach you about is what it will require from you to take habits. The answer to this is simple; it's self-discipline. In order to exert self-discipline, you also need to have willpower. A common belief in people is that they think they can change their lives for the better if they simply could just have more willpower. If people had more willpower, everyone would be able to start meditating every day, right? This is true to an extent; however, you will learn later in this chapter that you no longer need to exert willpower once an action becomes a habit. Let's take a look at what willpower is and how this will play into building new habits.

Willpower

In various scientific articles related to studies on willpower, it was reported that the biggest obstacle when it comes to people achieving change was the lack of willpower. Although many people often blame the scarcity of their willpower for their unhealthy choices, they are still grasping on to the hope of achieving it one day. Most people in this study also reported that they think willpower is something that can be taught and learned. They are absolutely correct. Some research recently has discovered many ways of how willpower can be strengthened with training and practice. On the contrary, some participants in the survey expressed that they think they would have more willpower if they had more free time to spare. However, the concept of willpower isn't something that increases automatically if a person has more time in their day. That leads me to the next question: How can people resist when they are faced with temptation? Over the last several years, scientists made many discoveries about how willpower works all over the world. We will dive a little deeper into what our current understanding of willpower is.

Weak willpower isn't the only reason for a person to fail at achieving their goals. Psychologists in the field of willpower have built three crucial components when it comes to achieving goals. They said that you first need to set a clear goal and then establish the motivation for change. They said the second component was to monitor your behavior in regards to that goal. Willpower itself is the third and final component. If your goal is similar to the following; stop smoking, get fit, study more, or stop wasting time on the internet, willpower is an important concept to understand if you are looking to achieve any of those goals.

The bottom line of willpower is achieving long-term goals by resisting temporary temptations and urges. Here are several reasons as to why this is beneficial. Over the course of a regular school year, psychologists performed a study that examined self-control in a class of eighth-grade students. The researchers in this study did an initial assessment of the self-discipline within the students by getting the students, their parents, and teachers to fill out a questionnaire. They took it one step further and gave these students the task of deciding whether they want to receive $1 right away or $2 if they waited a week. At the end of the study, the results pointed out that the students who had better test scores, better school attendance, better grades, and had a higher chance of being admitted to competitive high school programs all ranked high on the self-discipline assessment. These researchers found that self-discipline played a bigger role than IQ when it came to predicting academic success. Other studies have found similar evidence. In a different study, researchers asked a group of undergraduate university students to fill out self-discipline questionnaires that will be used to assess their self-control. These researchers developed a scale that helped score the student's in relation to the strength of their willpower. They found that the students that had higher self-esteem, better relationship skills, higher GPA, and had less alcohol or drug abuse all had the highest self-control scores from the questionnaire.

Another study found that the benefits of willpower tend to be relevant well past university years. This self-control study was conducted using a group of 1000 people who had been followed from birth to age 32. This is a long-term study in New Zealand where they wanted to learn more about the effects of self-control well into adulthood. They found that the people who had high self-control during their childhood grew up into adults that had better mental and physical health. They also had less likelihood of substance abuse, fewer criminal convictions, improved financial security, and better money-saving habits. These patterns were proven even after the researchers had adjusted external influences such as socioeconomic factors, general intelligence, and these people's home lives. These findings prove why willpower is extremely important in almost all areas of a person's life.

Now that you have learned the importance of willpower and its role in multiple stages of a person's life, let's define it a little further. Many other names are used for willpower that is used interchangeably; this includes; drive, determination, self-control, resolve, and self-discipline. Some psychologists will characterize willpower in even more specific ways. Some define willpower to be:

- The capacity to overcome unwanted impulses, feelings, or thoughts.
- The ability to resist temporary urges, temptation and delay instant gratification to achieve goals that are more long-term
- The effortful and conscious regulation of oneself.
- The capacity to engage a "cool" brain pattern instead of a "hot" brain pattern

- A limited resource that has the capability to be depleted

The Relationship Between Willpower and Meditation

A person makes decisions every day in order to resist urges and gratification so that they can seek a more healthy and happy long-term life. This could be in the form of refusing another portion of fries, forcing yourself to go work out, denying the second round of alcoholic drinks, or overcoming the temptation to skip early morning meetings. Willpower within everyone is always being put to the test.

Lack of willpower is one of the main obstacles in people's ability to maintain a healthy weight and physique. A lot of research actually supports this idea. A study found that kids who had more self-control were less likely to become overweight when they grew up into their adolescent years due to their ability to delay gratification and control their urges.

However, just like we talked about earlier, resisting those urges may diminish a person's willpower to resist the next temptation. A researcher proved this in a study where they offered students that were currently dieting some ice cream after watching a sad movie. Some of the participants were asked to watch the movie like any other normal day, while the other group was asked not to show any reactions or emotions, which is a task that requires self-control. The psychologists discovered that the participants who had to use their self-control to withhold their emotions and reactions indulged in more ice cream compared to the participants who were allowed to watch the movie normally and react as they'd like.

A lot of people often place most of the blame on their bad moods for causing their 'emotional eating.' However, that study found that the participants' emotional states were not the cause of the amount of ice cream that they consumed. In layman's terms, the depletion of willpower had more significance than a person's mood when it comes to determining how much ice cream the participants ate.

We have to keep in mind that the reason behind why someone is on a diet will also play a role in willpower depletion. As we had just discussed, researchers found that people's attitudes and inner beliefs may create a buffer for them in terms of the effects of willpower depletion. Another example based on this theory involved researchers asking participants to resist the temptation of eating cookies that were placed in front of them. He then tested the participant's strength of willpower by getting them to squeeze a handgrip until they couldn't anymore. Through this exercise, he discovered that those who refused the cookies for their own reasons (such as finding enjoyment in resisting treats) had better self-control in this physical test compared to the ones who refused the cookies for reasons that were external (wanting to impress the experimenter).

At this point, it is obvious that willpower is a required component when it comes to eating healthy. If a person is living in a surrounding where there are plenty of unhealthy but delicious food options, the action of resisting temptation is more likely to deplete willpower and even making it difficult for highly motivated healthy eaters. Since overeating behaviors are very complex, the role of willpower is argumentative when it comes to discussions for obesity treatments.

Some of the experts in the field of willpower believe that using self-control and personal choices causes people to be stigmatized, which makes them unlikely to be motivated to lose weight. Many dieticians advise against using willpower as a tool and argue that dieters should be focusing on lowering the effect that their environment will have on their eating habits and behavior. Ultimately, when it comes to the world we live in today, resisting the temptation to eat unhealthily can be a hard challenge. We are constantly exposed to ads for delicious high-calorie foods. Cheap and fast processed foods are available at our fingertips 24/7 and are less expensive compared to healthier options. A person's willpower and their external environment contribute to people's food-related choices. Understanding these two factors on a deeper level can prove useful in helping individuals and dieticians that are battling obesity.

Not only does willpower play a role in eating healthy, but it also plays a role in the use and possible abuse of alcohol, tobacco, and drugs. Children who have developed self-control may avoid substance abuse in their adulthood and teenagehood. Researchers in this field studied self-control in adolescents in their transition between sixth grade and eleventh grade. They discovered that kids with self-control problems in sixth grades, such as not speaking in turn during class, had more likelihood of using tobacco, marijuana, and alcohol as high schoolers.

This may not come as surprising, but willpower also plays a significant role in curbing alcohol abuse and usage. In another study, a researcher discovered that people who drank socially often that used their willpower during the lab proceeded to go out and consume more alcohol than the other participants who didn't use their willpower stockpile. In a different study, the researcher found that the social drinkers who had used a lot of their self-control that day were more likely to infringe on the drinking limits that they created for themselves. This finding shows evidence that exerting self-control excessively in one situation can cripple a person's ability to fight off other temptations in different parts of their life.

We are talking a lot about willpower because understanding the role it plays is very important for developing effective treatments and planning to battle serious issues like addictions to help guide people in making healthier choices for themselves. Willpower research offers people lots of suggestions on how to stick with healthy behaviors.

Improving Your Self-Control

Lots of research is being done recently in order to explain the numerous elements of willpower. Many professionals that study this area of self-control to this with one goal on their mind. They are about these types of questions: If willpower is a limited resource, what can we do to conserve it? How can we strengthen willpower?

One effective tactic for maintaining willpower is simply to avoid temptation. In the marshmallow study, children were given a choice to eat one marshmallow right away or have to wait an undefined period of time to have the opportunity to eat two marshmallows. They found that the kids who started at the marshmallows during the whole time were found to be less likely to resist the treat compared to the kids who shut their eyes and refused to look, looked away, or created a distraction for themselves. The technique of out of sight, out of mind, works with adults as well. In a recent study, researchers found that office workers who kept unhealthy snacks such as candy in their desk drawer consumed it less compared to when they would put the candy at eye level on the tables.

A technique called "implementation intention" is another helpful tactic that helps improve willpower. These intentions are usually in the form of "if-then" statements, which aid people in planning for environments that will pose a challenge in terms of disrupting their goals. For instance, a person monitoring their consumption of alcohol may tell themselves before entering a drinking part that if anybody offers them an alcoholic drink, they will request a plain soda with lime. Research has found that implementing solutions will increase self-control amongst adults and adolescents, even if people already had their willpower depleted by other tasks. People who have a plan going into it can more easily decide according to their goals, without needing to draw upon their bank of willpower resources.

This research suggests that people have a bank of willpower that is limited and raises a few troubling questions. Are people destined to fail if they are being faced with too many temptations? The answer is not necessarily. Many psychologists have the belief that a person's willpower cannot ever be used up completely. Instead, people often have stored some backup willpower that is being saved for future demands. Those reserves are only available for the right type of motivation, allowing them to accomplish things even when their willpower has seemingly run out.

In order to demonstrate this idea, a researcher further found out that individuals who had their willpower used up 'completely' continued to be able to accomplish self-control tasks when they were being told that they would be compensated well for their actions or if their actions would bring benefit to other people. He concluded that having high motivation can overcome weakened self-control.

Will power can also be controlled in the first place to be less vulnerable to being completely depleted. Psychologists often use an analogy to describe willpower as being similar to a muscle that will tire out after a lot of exercise. However, there is another element to this analogy. Although muscles will tire due to exercise during the short-term, they become stronger when regularly exercised over the long term. Just like physical exercise, self-control can become stronger when a person exercises willpower.

According to one of the earlier experiments that supports the idea above, the researchers asked participants in the study to follow a two-week guide to improve their moods, track their meal consumption, or ameliorate their physical posture. Compared to the group that didn't need to exercise self-control, the participants who had to use their willpower by performing heavy willpower exercises were not as vulnerable to the depletion of self-control in a follow-up study. In another set of research, this researcher showed people who smoke and who were asked to exercise willpower for 2 weeks (by resisting sweet foods or squeezing an exercise handgrip) found greater success when it comes to not smoking than other participants who were given tasks which didn't require any self-control.

Other researchers have also discovered that using your willpower muscles can help a person increase the strength of their self-control over a period of time. Some researchers in Australia did a study where they assigned participants to a physical exercise program that lasted two months; this is a willpower-required routine. In the conclusion of this program, the participants who finished it scored better when measuring self-control than the people who did not get the exercise program. The participants who did the program showed to have been smoking less, eating healthier food, drinking less alcohol, improving their study habits, and monitoring their spending habits more carefully. Regular exercise of a person's willpower using physical exercise seems to have led to an increase of willpower in their daily lives.

The research findings regarding how glucose levels are tied to willpower depletion suggest a conceivable solution. A person who maintains their blood sugar by eating regularly and often may help their brain replenish their willpower storage. Dieting aims to preserve their willpower while calorie reduction may be more effective by eating frequent and small meals compared to skipping out on entire meals like lunch or dinner.

All this evidence founded from studies of the depletion of willpower proposes that people making resolutions for the new year is the worst approach possible. If a person is running low on willpower in one specific area, it often reduces their willpower in all of the other areas. Focusing on one goal at a time makes more sense.

Therefore, it is less effective to begin a healthy diet right away. Instead, quit smoking and begin a new workout plan simultaneously. A much better technique is to complete goals one by one. Once you have one single good habit nailed, people no longer need to use their supply of willpower to uphold that action daily. Healthy habits eventually become a part of a person's daily routine and would not need to use decision-making energy at all.

There are still lots of areas of research to be done regarding willpower and its mechanisms in humans that need to see more research in the future. However, it seems like if somebody has clear and specific goals, an appropriate level of self-monitoring, and does a little bit of practice, they can train their self-control to be strong when faced with temptation.

How to Improve Your Self-Discipline

Now that you have an excellent understanding of the roles that willpower and habits will play on your ability to meditate, let's take a look at how you can improve your self-discipline to keep yourself on track. Improving your self-discipline is the only way for you to commit yourself to your meditation journey. Below are ten steps that will teach you how to improve your self-discipline so you can build new meditation habits.

1. Understanding your weaknesses.

Everyone has their own set of weaknesses. They could range from a certain type of food like chocolate, or it can be social media like Instagram, or even the latest addictive video game. Regardless of what it is, it has a similar effect on everyone.

The first step to mastering your self-discipline is to acknowledge your shortcomings, no matter what they might be. People often try to pretend that their weaknesses don't exist in order to portray themselves as a strong person. This is extremely ineffective when it comes to self-discipline. The purpose of acknowledging your weaknesses is not to make yourself feel bad; instead, it helps you recognize what they are and help you plan to overcome them. Acknowledge your flaws; it is impossible to overcome them until you do this.

2. Removing temptations

Once you have acknowledged your weaknesses, you can now move on to step two, which is to remove your temptations. Just like we mentioned in step one, everyone has their own set of weaknesses, and it can range from small things like an unhealthy snack all the way to something that hinders your productivity, like playing a video game for hours on end. By understanding your weaknesses, you can make accommodations for yourself that will help remove some of those temptations.

For example, if somebody is looking to lose weight and get fit at the gym, but they know that their weakness is that they always eat chocolate after dinner every night. In this case, their temptation removal would be to not buy any more chocolate that they keep around in their home. By not having chocolate in the home, they would be unable to fall into the temptation of eating it, which will hinder their progress of getting fit. However, this does not mean that they will never be able to eat chocolate again. This only means that they can indulge in their favorite snacks when they have achieved a certain portion of their goal. Rewarding oneself is important to self-discipline as well.

3. Set plans with goals for yourself

In order to continue strengthening your self-discipline, a person must have a clear vision of what goals they are trying to accomplish. They must also have an understanding of what success means to them. If a person doesn't know where they're planning to go or what accomplishing their goals even and Tails, it is easy for them to lose their way or to get sidetracked. Make sure the goals that you are setting have a clear and concise purpose.

4. Begin using self-discipline as practice

Self-discipline is not something that people are born with; it is mostly a learned behavior. Self-discipline is just like any other skill that people may be looking to grow; it requires repetition and lots of daily practice. Similar to going to the gym, the more you work out your muscles, the bigger and stronger they will become. Changes do not happen overnight; instead of strengthening your muscles and growing them, it will take at least several weeks for a person to see their progress. The effort and focus that training self-discipline requires can be extremely tiring.

The more time you practice self-discipline, it can become more and more difficult to keep utilizing your willpower. Sometimes when a person is faced with a big temptation or decision, they may feel that overcoming that large temptation makes it harder for them to overcome other tasks that also require self-discipline. The only way to move past this is to have a good mindset. Having a good mindset creates a buffer for how quickly your willpower becomes drained. In addition, like the muscle example we used, by exerting your willpower more often, you will have a higher tolerance and therefore be able to exert it more than if you were just starting out.

5. Keep your days simple, and start creating your new meditation habits.

To strengthen self-discipline, you need to work on instilling a new habit, which can feel very intimidating at first, especially if you are focusing on the entire goal all at once. To avoid this daunting feeling, keep it very simple. Break your bigger goal into smaller doable ones. Instead of trying to accomplish one huge goal all at once or to change all of your habits all at once, focus on doing just one thing consistently and exercise your self-discipline with that one small thing.

For example, if you are somebody that is looking to get into better shape, start by exercising for 10 to 15 minutes per day. Instead of trying to go to the gym for 2 hours every day, which can be very daunting, start with a smaller goal in mind first. By taking baby steps, you can get your mind used to that habit and slowly increase the amount of time that you spend at the gym. Eventually, once you feel like that goal has become a habit, you can then begin to focus on other small goals and keep building up words from there.

6. Implement a healthier diet

In the earlier chapters, we learned that glucose levels play a big role in a person's brainpower, which controls a person's willpower. The sensation of being hungry can cause people to feel angry, annoyed, and irritated. This feeling is real, and everyone has felt it before and often has a huge impact on a person's willpower. Research has found evidence that having low blood sugar weakens a person's ability to make good decisions.

When a person is hungry, their ability to concentrate suffers a lot, and their brains don't function optimally. Therefore, a person's self-control is likely to be weakened when their body is in this state. To prevent this, make sure to be eating small meals constantly to prevent yourself from feeling that annoying hungry feeling that causes people to have a lapse in judgment. Since exercising willpower takes up a lot of energy from a person's brain, make sure to keep fuelling it with enough glucose so that the brain is able to keep functioning at an optimal level.

7. Change your views surrounding willpower.

In the earlier chapters, we learned that a person's point of view or beliefs could create a buffer of how long it takes to have their willpower drained completely. Although most researchers believe that there is a limit to how much we can tap into our willpower, they also found that the people who believe that there wasn't a limit had a bigger willpower stockpile. If a person believes that they have a limited amount of willpower, they probably will not be able to surpass those limits. However, if a person does not place a strict limit on themselves, they are less likely to use up their willpower stockpile before meeting their goals. A person's internal perception about their own willpower and self-control plays a huge role in determining how much willpower they have. If a person can remove these obstacles by believing that they have a large stockpile of willpower and believing in themselves, they are less likely to drain out their willpower than someone who believes that they don't have much of it. So try changing your own perception of how you see your willpower. Try to think of it as a source that can run out, but you have a larger amount of it because of your beliefs. This is a much better mindset than thinking that willpower will run out, so you should be stingy with it.

8. Create a backup plan

Many psychologists use a famous technique that helps with boosting willpower called "implementation intention." This technique is where you give yourself a plan when you are faced with a potentially difficult situation. We used this example earlier, wherein a person is trying to reduce the amount of alcohol that they drink. They know that they are going to a party where they will be asked if they want to drink alcohol; instead of always asking for a beer like they normally do, they will instead ask for a plain soda with lime.

By making a plan before going to a situation that you know where you will be confronted with big temptations, you will have an action plan where you can automatically use rather than have to come up with an excuse on the spot and risking failure. When a person goes into those situations with a plan, it helps give them the mindset and self-control necessary to overcome obstacles. They will be able to save energy by not having to make sudden decisions or make sudden plans based on their emotional state. This will make them less likely to cave into temptations and more likely to exercise their self-discipline.

9. Reward yourself

Like anything else in life, it is necessary to give yourself a break and reward yourself. Give yourself something to look forward to by planning an appropriate reward when you accomplish your goals. This is not much different from when you were a little kid, and you got a treat from your parents for showing good behavior. When a person has something to look forward to, it gives them the extra motivation that they need to succeed.

Anticipation is a powerful thing. It gives people something to focus on so that they are not only thinking of all the things that they need to change. When you have achieved one of your goals, you can find yourself a new goal and a new reward in order to keep motivating yourself to move forward. However, the reward should not be something unhealthy. For example, in the previous example of the person that is trying to lower their alcohol intake, their reward for not drinking as often should not be that they will go binge drinking next Friday. Their awards should be something healthy that won't make them lose progress on all the work that they've done.

10. Forgive yourself for lapses.

Even if a person has all the best intentions and the most well-made plans, sometimes they will fall short when practicing self-discipline. Avoiding failure altogether is impossible, and we should not build a mindset around that. Everyone will have their ups and downs, their successes and their failures. The key to overcoming the failures that you will face is simply to keep moving forward. If you stumble on your journey of self-discipline, instead of giving up altogether, acknowledge what caused it, learn from it, and then move on. Don't let yourself get caught up in frustration, anger, or guilt because these emotions are the ones that will de-motivate you and get in the way of your future progress. Learn from the mistakes you have made and be comfortable with forgiving yourself. Once you have done that, you can get your head back in the game and start where you left off.

Appendix 1: The Meditator's Diet

As we discussed in earlier chapters, healthy habits such as diet are crucial for those who are pursuing a meditation journey. Ensuring that you are nourishing your body as much as you are your mind is a critical step in meditation. In this chapter, I will be spending some time teaching you about the meditator's diet. I will also be teaching you other healthy habits that you can implement to add additional health and value to your meditation journey.

A Typical Buddhist Meditation Practioner's Diet

Buddhist monks are known for their basic diets of eating whatever is served to them without complaint. This may not be realistic for modern-day meditators but having a similar type of healthy diet proves to be crucial in the world of meditation.

Think about how your mind and your body are very connected. If you worry, you begin to feel the emotion of anxiety; if you experience this emotion for too long, you begin showing physical symptoms. By improving your physical health, it can work in reverse, where putting the right nutrients and vitamins into your body can help your mind feel healthier too.

Research has proven that making healthier changes in an individual's diet can make substantial changes in one's general mood or sense of wellbeing. Although it is not a complete substitute treatment, it is a great way to complement whatever treatments an individual is taking to reduce anxiety, stress, and depression. Here are a few tips that you can take to achieve a more well-balanced diet.

- Include some protein in your breakfast. Having protein at breakfast helps many people feel fuller and for longer. It helps keep blood sugar steady and helps give you more energy at the beginning of the day.
- Opt for complex carbohydrates. Research has found evidence that carbohydrates increase serotonin amount in the brain, which produces a calming effect. Opt for foods that are rich in complex carbs such as quinoa, oatmeal, whole-grain cereals, and whole-grain bread. Try to avoid foods that contain simple carbohydrates like sugary drinks and foods.
- Increase your water consumption. Even the mildest dehydration can cause symptoms like irritability and dry mouth, which is enough to negatively affect a person's mood.

If you are someone that's been experiencing a lot of anxiety, being mindful of what you are eating can help mitigate some of those feelings. Some of the newest research suggests that specific foods can help reduce anxiety based on the nutrients they bring. Here is a list of suggested foods and how they can help reduce anxiety:

- Brazil Nuts: This type of nut is high in the element selenium. Selenium is proven to improve mood because it reduces inflammation, which is often at increased levels if someone is suffering from an anxiety or mood disorder. Certain soybeans, mushrooms, and nut products are also a good source of selenium. Keep in mind not to consume too much selenium as there can be side effects. The recommended limit for adults is 400 mcg per day.
- Fatty Fish: Trout, salmon, sardines, herring, and mackerel are all fish that are high in omega-3. Omega-3 is a fatty acid that has been proven recently to have a strong link with improving cognitive function and mental health. Foods that contain lots of Omega-3 provide two essential fatty acids, EPA and DHA. EPA and DHA are great at reducing inflammation and promoting healthy brain function.

- Vitamin D: Much research links vitamin D deficiency to disorders like anxiety and depression. There has been enough evidence over the years to prove that vitamin D improves depression and anxiety. It can also be used to improve other disorders like seasonal disaffected disorder during winter times.
- Eggs: Egg yolks contain a lot of vitamin D and are also a great source of protein. Since it is a complete protein, it contains the necessary amino acids for your body's growth and development. Eggs also contain an amino acid called tryptophan, which aids in the creation of serotonin.
- Pumpkin Seeds: Pumpkin seeds are a superb source of potassium, which is responsible for regulating electrolytes and managing blood pressure. Potassium-rich foods are proven to reduce symptoms of anxiety and stress.
- Dark chocolate: Dark chocolate is an excellent source of magnesium. Magnesium has been proven to reduce symptoms of depression and anxiety. Dark chocolate is also high in tryptophan, which helps with serotonin production.

- Turmeric: Turmeric contains an active ingredient called curcumin, which lowers anxiety from its inflammation-reducing ability.
- Chamomile: Chamomile has properties of anti-inflammation, antioxidant, antibacterial, and relaxant. Chamomile has been proven to reduce various anxiety symptoms.
- Yogurt: Yogurt contains many healthy bacteria that have been proven to have positive effects on the health of the brain. Due to its anti-inflammatory effects, yogurt has been proven to reduce the inflammation that is partially responsible for depression, stress, and anxiety.
- Green Tea: Green tea contains theanine, which is a type of amino acid. It has calming and anti-anxiety effects and promotes the production of serotonin and dopamine.

Just like how many foods aid in reducing inflammation that has been proved to be linked to enhancing symptoms of anxiety, other foods do the opposite. Moreover, foods that contain high sugars can lead to a feeling of jitteriness or hyperactivity. Like caffeine, high sugars can emphasize anxiety symptoms, which can make an individual feel worse. Here are a few foods that you should try to avoid in order to manage your anxiety symptoms:

- Fruit Juice: Fruit juice is mostly sugar water that works quickly to make you feel hyper but will bring you down just as fast. It often leaves people feeling hungry, which worsens symptoms of anxiety. Try to opt for whole food instead of processed food as the fiber works well to fill you up and slow down the intake of energy into your blood, which reduces hyperactivity.
- Soda: Similar to fruit juice, soda contains a ton of sugar, which will cause a similar hyper to crash effect as fruit juice. Research has proven that sugary drinks have a direct link to anxiety and depression. Try to opt for soda water with a splash of juice to satisfy the craving without consuming the sugar.
- White Bread: White bread is made from highly processed white flour that turns into blood sugar when you eat it. It causes energy spikes and crashes that emphasize the symptoms of anxiety and depression. Opt for whole-grain bread (not whole wheat as sometimes it is just white bread dyed brown).
- Salad Dressing: Pre-packed salad dressing often contains a ton of sugar

due to the use of high fructose corn syrup. This can also cause energy spikes and crashes.

- Ketchup: Ketchup is made of mostly sugar and can lead to an energy spike and crash. Even ketchup that is advertised as 'light' contains artificial sweeteners that have been proven to be linked to depression and anxiety. Opt for homemade salsa instead to limit the sugar intake.
- Processed Foods: Processed foods contain a lot of sugar or other preservatives that have been related to enhancing the symptoms of anxiety and depression. This includes refined cereals, fried foods, pastries, candy, and high-fat dairy products.

Other Healthy Habits to Consider

Let's take a look at a few exercises and habits that will help you improve your physical mindfulness. Begin by incorporating one of these exercises into your daily routine and begin to incorporate more when they have become habits. By slowly incorporating all of these exercises, you will find that you have become more mindful of your physical health and your body's feelings.

1. Taking daily breaks and 'time outs'

Making the time to take a couple of 'time outs' each day is crucial in letting an individual's mind rest from all the mental exercise. You can do this by scheduling at least one 15-minute block a day where you find somewhere quiet and private to sit by yourself. During this time, you can practice something that can ground you into the present to help you focus on that rather than the whirlwind of thoughts caused by anxiety. For example, you can take this time to do quick mindfulness meditation, breathing exercises, or simply go for a walk. Mindfulness meditation can help you bring your awareness to the present and notice your surroundings, which then takes you away from all the worries running through your mind. Breathing exercises are very useful in not only calming your body down but also helps you stay focused by practicing your breathing patterns. If you may not have the privacy or opportunity to do those things, you can opt to just go for a walk. However, keep in mind that you should not be speeding through the process on this walk. Try to incorporate mindfulness by focusing on the things around you, such as the people, noise, smells, and buildings. Pay attention to what's around you and try to see if you notice things around you that you've never noticed before. Taking these timeouts every day will help give your mind a break from the constant worrying and give you the opportunity to focus on the present.

2. Avoiding alcohol and caffeine

Caffeine is a stimulant that gives someone jittery effects similar to the feelings of those experiencing a frightening event. Caffeine actually triggers our natural flight or fight response and can make existing anxiety worse or, in serious cases, trigger a panic attack. Moreover, having too much caffeine can even make a non-anxious person feel nervous or moody. Anxiety is mindfulness's worst enemy; with anxious feelings present, it is difficult to be mindful of the present.

Alcohol has always been strongly linked to anxiety. Lots of research has proven that individuals who suffer from anxiety disorders are 2-3 times more likely to have problems with drugs or alcohol. Opposite from caffeine, alcohol is a depressant and can make certain symptoms of anxiety feel even worse. Many people with anxiety disorders turn to alcohol as self-treatment because of its immediate calming effects. However, as your body begins to process this alcohol, it often makes people feel edgy and commonly interferes with sleep. Moreover, alcohol dehydrates a person's body significantly, which creates symptoms of dehydration, which are similar to the symptoms of anxiety. It can also cause hangovers, which can further debilitate someone who is suffering from a mental disorder. Long story short, if you are someone who is suffering from a mental disorder, cutting out alcohol is a good first step.

3. Incorporating more exercise

Although most people relate physical exercise to improve physical health, many studies have proven that exercise is absolutely necessary for maintaining mental health. Exercise helps to reduce stress, fatigue and improves concentration and overall cognitive function. This is particularly helpful when stress has depleted an individual's overall energy or ability to concentrate. Biologically, when stress begins to affect one's brain, the nerve connections affect the rest of the body to feel that impact as well. Vice versa, when your body feels better, your mind does too. Exercise helps your body produce endorphins (your body's natural painkillers) and improves the ability and quality of sleep, which then helps reduce stress.

Psychologists that have studied the relationship between exercise and anxiety suggest that a 10-minute walk every day can be as good as a 45-minute workout. Other studies showed that exercise works quickly and can help improve a depressed or anxious person's mood. The effects may be temporary, but a brisk walk or a simple workout can provide hours of relief. More research has shown that physically active individuals have lower anxiety and depression rates than sedentary people.

4. Improving your sleeping habits

If an individual is experiencing stress, worry, or anxiety, they have a very chance of struggling to achieve a healthy sleep cycle. They may have trouble falling asleep or staying asleep during the night. A vigorous mental activity like worrying tends to keep the brain from settling down, which causes the inability to fall asleep or stay asleep. Lack of sleep then causes an individual to feel more on edge the next day.

There are a few ways of how an individual can tackle their sleep problems. First, they can incorporate exercise to tire the body out and clear the mind of mental activity. They can also try to improve their diet, which leads to a better balance of nutrition that can aid with improving sleep quality. Here are a few tips on how to improve sleep in order to manage anxiety:

- Exercise: Exercise has been directly linked to lower symptoms of anxiety and sleep improvement. It can help readjust your sleeping cycle and can treat illnesses like insomnia or sleep apnea.
- Tailor Your Environment: Different people have different requirements of how they prefer their sleeping environment. By controlling things like temperature, sound, and light can help people get a good night's rest. The majority of people find that keeping the

bedroom darker, cooler, and quieter helps achieve a better night's sleep.

- Avoiding Caffeine and Alcohol: As we mentioned previously, caffeine causes jitteriness, which can get in the way of falling or staying asleep. Alcohol also increases the heart rate, which is a culprit in keeping people awake. Instead of drinking caffeine and alcohol often, try drinking plain water to stay hydrated to promote healthier sleep.
- Calming Your Mind: Limiting the amount of mental activity in your brain before sleep can help improve the time it takes you to fall asleep and the actual sleep quality. Try some relaxation techniques like mindfulness or breathing exercises as you go to bed to keep your mind calm. Practicing these techniques in the day also helps you apply them easier at night.
- Limiting Screen Time: The light that emits from our electronics keeps our minds awake, which is detrimental when you are trying to fall asleep. Try to limit your screen time before you go to bed. Things like checking work emails or social media can trigger worries and stress that will keep your mind active all night.

An unhealthy sleeping schedule can cause a person a lot of anxiety, which will slow down or even prevent their process of achieving mindfulness. Improving your overall sleep cycle will keep your mind fresh and decrease the risk of generating anxious thoughts.

5. Socialize more often

Humans are innately a social species. Throughout our generations, being social has helped humans thrive and survive. One of the reasons for this is that humans are innately compassionate living beings, and we need to satisfy that in order to feel fulfilled. When you take away socialization, humans naturally tend to feel unfulfilled and lonely. By making an effort to go out into the world and be around others, people can begin to feel like they are a part of society. Social activities decrease the feeling of loneliness while promoting those of enjoyment, belonging, security, and safety.

Socialization is proven to directly impact our anxiety and stress levels in several ways. First, socialization promotes a hormone responsible for decreasing anxiety levels and makes us feel more confident in our ability to cope with anxiety and stress. It also encourages us to spend our energy outwards rather than inwards. Often, when people are focused on reaching out to others, they are distracted from their own stress, pain, or circumstances. When people spend time socializing, they actually strengthen their sense of 'life has meaning and purpose' and ultimately increases their mood. Here are a few things you can do to try to increase your socialization:

- Initiate social interactions with friends or family. Do things like talk on the phone, eat at a restaurant, have a party, or even exercise together.
- Introduce yourself to people you come in contact with often, like your neighbors.
- Join classes or groups that interest you (exercise groups, hobby groups...etc.)

Do bear in mind that it is quality socialization that counts rather than quantity if you surround yourself with many people that you don't know that well is not as effective as surrounding yourself with 2 - 3 close friends/family to socialize with.

Conclusion

Thank you for making it through to the end of this meditation guide. I hope it was informative and able to provide you with all of the tools you need to achieve your meditation goals. There is a whole lot of information for you to take in as there are so many different types and ways to perform meditation. Simply just meditating is not enough to help a person truly become mindful. You have to implement different types of mindfulness in different areas of your life. For instance, one person could have mastered the art of mindfulness using yoga, but they may have no idea how to implement mindfulness anywhere else in their life. This book is filled with many different mindfulness topics to help you combat this problem. It will prevent you from getting pigeon-holed into one area of mindfulness, and it will help you distribute mindfulness evenly throughout various areas of your life.

True masters of mindfulness and meditation are able to be mindful at any time of the day. They don't require meditation sessions or worksheets, or a therapist to help them with this. They have already implemented mindfulness into their daily habit with every single task and thought they have and do. This book is filled with exercises and ideas of how you can practice mindfulness, but at the end of the day, it is completely up to you to practice mindfulness without the help of exercises and worksheets. These worksheets and exercises are here to help you learn mindfulness, but they are not here to help you become mindful every minute of the day. Only you are able to control that, and your own self-discipline is what is going to help you achieve your goal.

The first step for you is to continue to practice mindfulness by following the exercises and meditations provided in this book. Take it slow and once you feel like you have mastered a certain exercise, try to do that exercise during your daily tasks. For instance, if you feel like you have mastered mindfulness meditation, try to practice this meditation while driving or cooking. By combining new mindfulness exercises into various tasks and activities in your life, you are implementing them as a part of your daily routine. If you continue to do this on a daily basis, you will accomplish your goal of incorporating meditation and mantras into your life. I wish you the best of luck on your journey, and I urge you not to give up.

Pranayama Breathing Techniques Book

Mark Gabriel Reynolds

Introduction to Yoga Pranayama

I want to thank you for choosing this book on pranayama breathing. I hope that you find the information informative and helpful. Throughout this book, we will be discussing pranayama breathing and how it can help you live a healthier life. Pranayama is one of the most important aspects of yoga, and these techniques can be used daily in your personal lives.

At one time, breath, mind, ear, eye, and tongue were arguing about who was the best and who was the most important to live. They asked their father, the Lord-of-Creation, for his opinion. Prajapati gave them a simple method to settle this problem, "He by whose departure the body seems worse than worst, he is the best of you."

The tongue then left a year, and when he returned, he asked them how they had lived. They told him, "Like mute people, not speaking." They could still breathe, hear, and think just fine. Then the eye left. He asked the same question as tongue upon his return. The others replied, "Like blind people, not seeing."

The body could still breathe, think, hear, and talk.

Then ear left, and upon his return, he was told, "Like deaf people, not hearing." Still, the body could breathe, think, see, and talk. Off went the mind, and when he returned, they told him, "Like children whose mind is not yet formed." The body could still breathe, hear, see, and talk just fine.

Lastly, breath got ready to leave. Immediately, the others realized there was no way they could live without breath. "Madam," they all cried out, "you are the best. Do not leave us." This is why people don't call these five the Vital Minds, Vital Ears, Vital Eyes, or Vital Tongues, but, instead, they call it the Vital Breaths. Vital Breath is all of these things.

I tell you that story to highlight the reason for this book. Without breath, we will cease to exist. We can live without our tongue, ears, eyes, or mind. While life might not be easy without those things, it is still livable. Without breath, we die. Breath is our life, but we humans aren't breathing as we should.

You may or may not be versed in yoga. If you do have experience with yoga, then you

probably know some postures or asanas. Even in yoga, pranayama has taken a backseat to the vigorous practice of learning asanas.
Historically, it was the other way around. In yoga schools that teach both and not every one of them does, asana is mainly used to prepare people for the time-consuming and advanced practice of pranayama. While most of the time, pranayama is translated as "breath control," and while this is slightly accurate, it doesn't give you the whole story of what pranayama is.

This book will take you through the process of learning about pranayama breathing and how to start your breathing practice. I want you to understand the importance of this breathing practice, and that's why we will go over the history of pranayama and how it can benefit your mind and body.

Then we will move into the importance of correct breathing. Breathing may have been the first thing we did when we came into this world, aside from crying, but we have forgotten how to breathe properly. This will also look at the different postures you can sit in when working with your breath. Please remember, though, these postures are less important than the proper breath.

After that, you will learn all about different pranayama breaths. There isn't just one, and in fact, this book probably doesn't even cover all of them. Each breath can help you in various ways, so you can choose which breath cycle you feel will help you the most.

Even though teaching about pranayama breathing is the main purpose of this book, I will leave you with one last thing. We will go over a yoga diet. We'll look at sex, sleep, and food, along with the four primitive urges. Combined with your pranayama breathing practice, all of this will guide you towards living a full and healthy life. Let us begin.

Chapter 1: Pranayama Breathing

Most people charge their cell phones when they go to bed each night, but how can we recharge our minds? The best and easiest way might just be in your breathing.

Pranayama comes from a Sanskrit word that describes yoga breathing exercises that can improve physical health, mental clarity, release stress, and increase energy. The word "breathwork" is a recent term that is used to describe pranayama or breathing exercises. Yoga is an ancient Indian system that declares prana as being the energy or universal life force that distinguishes the dead from the living. This energy or life force flows through energy channels known as Nadi and the chakra's energy centers.

Prana is a vital energy that we need in our subtle and physical layers, and if we don't have it, we will die. Prana is what keeps us living.

Prana has various meaning levels, from consciousness energy to our physical breath to our creative power given birth to kundalini shakti. Yogis will tell you that the whole universe was created from prana.

Prana is a bit tricky to understand since we can't see it. But we can feel it. Having a clear awareness of what prana is and isn't, you can be so connected that you can feel the prana. Once we can connect to prana, we will connect with the world and who we truly are.
Even though prana relates to the breath, it isn't our actual breath. It's an energy that travels throughout the body through a network of channels. You could compare it to the central nervous system. All of these channels connect everything within the mind and body and behave like a conduit for prana.

There are over 3000 years that reference to prana that has transcended spiritual traditions and cultures. Prana has been a central part of tantric yoga, hatha yoga, ayurvedic, and Hindu traditions, but they all refer to the "life force." The Hebrew's ruah, the Islamic's ruh, the pneuma of ancient Greeks, the anima or ancient Romans, and the Chinese chi can be seen in the Christian's Holy Spirit.

Even though it might not be the same as breathing, prana can be described as respiration or breath. More definitions include soul, spirit, inner winds, vital winds, spiritual energy, or life force.

Some traditions have found between five and ten various prana kinds that relate to downward, upward, outward, and inward moving energy or energy that relates to specific places within the body like the digestion, heart, throat, or head.

Every human has a body. We also have an energetic body and a physical shape. Our active body is sometimes called the subtle body. It is what some people refer to as an aura since it extends further than our bodies. You've heard the saying, "they light up a room." This is where that saying comes from. It is how we sense another person's energy.

This subtle body has a central nervous system made up of nadis or channels made up of one central channel, and two side channels, which some refer to as the moon and sun, and 72,000 smaller channels. Depending on the tradition, there might be more than 72,000 channels.

The sun channel, or Pingala, travels up the right of the spine. It is represented by "ha" in Sanskrit. This is a red channel where ignorant disliking, aversions, separateness, jealousy, and anger like to live. All of their "hot" energies have been associated with the sun.
As this energy travels through the Pingala channel on the exhale, we could experience rejection. Ignorant disliking can be labeled like this since we think that removing specific things or people from our lives will bring us happiness. But a wise person knows that happiness only comes from inside us.

The moon channel, or ida, runs up the left of the spine. It is represented by "tha" in Sanskrit. All the cooler energies flow through this channel like ignorant liking, attachment, cravings, and desires.
When prana moves upward when we inhale, our mind gets attracted to any object that we desire. It "ignorantly" craves what it thinks will make us happy. A wise person knows that

happiness comes from within, and happiness that will last isn't found in people or objects.

Found right in front of the spine is the avadhuti, Sushumna, shaking channel, singing channel, or central channel. Its name refers to the hum we feel when we feel true bliss that comes upi when prana can freely flow through the Nadi.

The ultimate goal of the "ha-tha" yoga is to move the "ha" and "tha" energies out of the side channels and into the central channel. "Hatha" yoga was initially practiced to pull and push the inner breath into the central channel by manipulating the physical body.
If prana freely flows in this central channel, we have reached Samadhi, which is considered full integration. This is characterized by feelings of contentment, pure joy, and wisdom.

These channels wrap around and work together in various central points throughout the body. These are known as "wheels," and we know them as chakras. These charkas cross the central channel could turn into choke points and could block prana movement. When you hear that somebody has a blocked chakra, this central channel has been gummed up by something within one of the chakras.

The exact number and placement of the chakras vary in every tradition. Most Hindu traditions say there are either seven or six chakras, while Buddhists say there are five.

Meditation and yoga can unblock these points by transferring some of the prana moving in the side channels into that central channel. When you are physically doing yoga, you might feel an electric charge as it goes through your body. Anytime you get a "gut feeling" or "a shiver," you are responding to your sixth sense.

You could see what prana is doing by simply watching your breath. When prana's electricity moves through the right channel, it will exit through your right nostril. During this time, the left, logical part of the brain will become activated. If you activate the left nostril, the right and creative part of the brain is more dominant.

Usually, there is only one side of the nostril that is more dominant than the other, which changes each hour. If you have reached a state of complete absorption, samadhi, or nirvana when you meditate, you will be able to breathe equally out both nostrils simultaneously. You don't have energy flowing through the side channels.

One of the best ways to connect to the prana is to note certain sensations you feel when you breathe. It isn't an accident that we relate our inhale to vibrant feelings, awake feelings, greater energy, and happiness. When we exhale our breath, we are breathing out disappointments, sadness, and letting go of the bad things in life. The cycle of sadness and happiness, impermanent and constantly changing, is a cycle that we stay within while we are breathing.
When yoga pulls, pushes, and moves the inner breath toward the central channel by physically manipulating the body, meditation does the same thing by influencing the mind. Ancient texts will say that a person's thoughts right their prana like a person rides a horse. Because of this, you can guide your prana using your thoughts and move them to the center channel.

By pranayama and meditation, we will learn how to control our breath. Most people have noticed when meditation gets interrupted, and our breathing does too. If our meditation is resting and calm, we won't be able to notice our breath.

Because breath and thoughts are connected, they can change by focusing on just one. One of the yoga limbs is controlling your breath by using exercises to manipulate your prana by using asana and meditation. Properly used pranayama techniques can cure illnesses and keep us healthy. There are many different techniques out there that can help us increase our energy, calm and clear our minds, and warm the body. One study done in 2012 shows that doing the ujjayi technique can turn off our stress response.

By combining pranayama, meditation, and asana, your Kundalini energy lying dormant at the base of your spine will begin to travel upward through that central channel. It will then be released through the crown chakra, bringing your enlightenment. For some, this will only happen as soon as they die when our prana gets sent to the heart chakra and then release through the crown.

Since prana is a universal energy that just doesn't exist inside us, we aren't separated from the fire's, water's, earth's, and wind's energy throughout the entire world. Our inside breath is related to the breath outside.

While we practice being aware of the prana in our breath and body, we could practice noticing how energy moves in the world around us and affects the environment and weather and how the intoxicants, caffeine, and foods we consume affect our energy.

Being aware of prana and our subtle body takes us a lifetime. During meditation, being aware of thoughts provides the right conditions to respond wisely. Being aware of the gifts that prana gives us is the same ability. With time and developing a better awareness, we can intentionally move energy toward the central channel and experience contentment and bliss that can never be disturbed.

There are several sources to sustain, maintain, and increase the level of your prana. You could classify these into four main categories: calmness, breath, rest, and food.

You will find more prana in fresh foods that you will in stale or canned foods. The foods that vegetarians eat are higher in prana, but since meat is dead, it is considered negative or extremely low prana.

The best source of prana is your breath. If your breathing stops, you will die. As I will go over in a few minutes, how we breathe can profoundly affect the way we feel.

It was found that the quality and quantity of prana and how it flows through the energy channels can determine our state of mind.

Because we don't pay enough attention to our energy channels, they might become a bit blocked, making the flowing prana jerky or broken. This could result in having negative emotions, doubts, depression, tension, conflict, uncertainty, fear, and worry.
If our prana levels are high and can flow in a steady, smooth, and continuous motion, our minds will be enthusiastic, positive, happy, and calm.
The ancient yoga scriptures mention and define various pranayama techniques.

The *Patanjali Yoga Sutra 2.49* gives pranayama the definition of: "In that state of being in asana or posture, breaking the usual movement of inhalation or exhalation is regulation of breath."

This means that prana is the universal life force and that Ayama works to lengthen or regulate it.
These ancient yogis noticed how powerful the breath was, and it could increase a person's prana. So they created a special breathing

technique that was able to increase a person's energy, create calmness, maintain health, and clear their mind so that they could meditate better.

Pranayama isn't a way to control your breathing, as some people think, but it helps you control your prana or energy with your breath. Those techniques involve breathing through your nostrils in a pattern where you will inhale, hold your breath, and exhale. Some of the most common breathing exercises include Nadi Shodhan, Bhramari pranayama, and Bhastrika pranayama.

If these are done right, pranayama could bring harmony to the spirit, mind, and body while being supervised. This makes you spiritually, mentally, and physically strong.

History of Pranayama

This timeline will give you an overview of pranayama's history and its practices. Even though this list isn't intended to be comprehensive or exhaustive, it does include some ket texts that might interest anybody who wants to know more about pranayama's history.

"Brihadaranyaka Upanishad – 700 BCE"

While the word prana was discovered in Chandogya Upanishad as early as 3000 CBE, information referring to a breathing practice that they call pranayama didn't happen until a lot later, somewhere around 700 BCE.

The earliest recorded reference to pranayama breathing can be found in the *Brihadaranyaka Upanishad* in hymn 1.5.23. This links breathing to regulating our life force.

There aren't any other guidelines for practicing pranayama in the *Upanishad*. But the idea that breathing can help a person reach immortality and better health is repeated continuously throughout yogic teachings and texts.

"The Bhagavad Gita – 5th Century to 2nd Century BCE."

You can also find pranayama mentioned in the *Bhagavad Gita*. The text in chapter four and verse 29 highlights using conscious exhaling, inhaling, and breath retention to get into a trancelike state. This text also says that practicing pranayama regularly can help a person gain more control over their sense by "curtailing the eating process."

"The *Maitrayaniya Upanishad* – Fourth Century BCE"

This is probably the essential pranayama text because it houses the earliest reference to pranayama as one part of a bigger, multifaceted system. It was probably written hundreds of years before the Yoga Sutras of Patanjali, which taught about union, reasoning, meditation, concentration, sensory withdrawal, and breath control used in yoga.

Pranayama is mentioned explicitly in chapter six and verse 21. It explains that you can reach deliverance by using different breathing retentions while concentrating on saying "Om" to help prana flow into the energy channels.

"Patanjali's Yoga Sutras – 100 to 400 CE"

Many scholars will agree that this text is a compilation of texts from all the earlier yogis. By the time Patanjali became a yogi, yoga has adapted and grown to extreme measures. Where the *Maitrayaniya Upanishad* has spoken of the six-limbed system, it became expanded to an eight-limbed system, which included niyama, asana, Yama, and pranayama with four other stages of meditative absorption that are Samadhi, dhyana, Dharana, and pratyahara.

This text references pranayama in verses 2.29 through 2.53 in the Sutras. While Patanjali doesn't dive deep into what prana is, it details some aspects of the breath like retention, exhales, and inhale. It also talks about pranayama in verse 2.51 that explains that it goes beyond all of the others.

Plus, it notes several benefits of practicing pranayama. Some of these benefits include better concentration and better physical fitness. Concentration is a deeper state of yoga. Within verse 2.52, it talks about how a pranayama practice can dissolve or lessen the veil that covers the "inner illumination."

Benefits of Pranayama

The key to having a happy and healthy life might just lie in how you breathe. If you can learn to attend to your breath, it can bring you back to the present, make you feel calmer, and make you more aware of yourself.

Pranayama can purify the nadis or psychic channels and enables mental and physical stability. It can purify over 72,000 channels within the body. It can purify the respiratory and blood systems. Deep breathing can enrich the blood with oxygen. Vast amounts of oxygen will get to the capillaries, heart, lungs, and brain.

Pranayama takes it one step more than just being aware of your breath. It uses certain techniques and rhythms to give you several benefits in your physical, emotional, and mental states.

- Could slow down the aging
- Rejuvenates the mind and body
- Immune system booster
- It brings positivity and enthusiasm
- Increases energy
- It gets rid of brain fog
- Improves attention and focus
- Reduces anxiety and worries
- Calms the mind

Pranayama techniques can help treat a large range of disorders related to stress like:

- Improving physical fitness by practicing specific yoga asanas
- It can help with weight loss

- Changes the cardiorespiratory system and helps lower blood pressure
- It helps get rid of unnecessary thoughts that can calm down your overactive mind that help reduce depression and anxiety
- It helps relieve asthma symptoms
- Improve autonomic functions
- Breathing deeply while focusing on your breath could be very rejuvenating and relaxing.
- Doing this regularly can improve your state of mind, memory, and concentration

Psychology Today described breathing as "an incredible alternative to mindfulness you never heard of." They also said it "could help those of us who can't be inactive because it is an active meditation."
There have been more than 65 studies done on combining Sudarshan kriya and pranayama breathing. They demonstrated many different health benefits.

Regulates Emotions

Pranayama breathing can help a person regulate their emotions. In a conference held in Germany, the founder of the "Art of Living

Foundation," Sri Sri Ravi Shankar, explained how emotions and breathing are connected.

- If we know our breath's rhythm, we can control our mind, we could handle negative emotions such as greed, jealousy, and anger, while we are smiling from the heart.

- If you work with a theatre group, you know that when a director asks you to begin breathing faster, you can show that you are angry. If you need to show a calm and serene mind, you will be told to breathe slow and soft.

- The breath has been linked to emotions. There will be a certain rhythm to the breath for each emotion. Even though we can't harness the actual feeling, you can handle them with your breathing.

One study done by Phillipot showed that breathing patterns that mimic happiness, sadness, and anger, can create the same emotional state inside us.
This is the principle that pranayama works with. Instead of letting our emotions change our breathing patterns, we could change the state of our emotions by being able to use our

breath skillfully. Since it is hard to control emotions, if we use pranayama techniques to change negative and overpowering emotions, it can turn into a powerful tool to enhance our inner peace and well being.

Shallow or Deep Breathing

Take a minute right now and become aware of your breath. Is it choppy, smooth, shallow, or deep? You can learn the right way to breathe by watching how newborn babies breathe. Have you noticed how their bellies rise and fall gently while they breathe in and out?

Most adults breathe from their chest. This type of breathing is shallow, and it sends the brain a signal that we are stressed, and something is wrong. But if we can learn to breathe deeply from our belly, it can boost respiration, making sure a good supply of oxygen gets to our brain and tells it that everything is fine.

Take another minute and become aware of your breathing one more time. Since you have been thinking about it, has it got any smoother or longer?

Difference Between Breathing Exercises and Pranayama

Many people call pranayama breathing exercises but not every breathing exercise can be called pranayama. Most breathing exercises aren't pranayama. Pranayama means "expansion of life force and its purpose is to improve the body's capacity to retain and increase prana in the body."

If we want to increase our ability to keep prana, doing pranayama exercises can cleanse our nadis or energy channels. By regularly practicing pranayama, these channels can become purer, and our bodies can retain more prana, and our minds can meditate and concentrate better. Regularly practicing pranayama can awaken our inner spiritual force, bring joy while enhancing spiritual development.

To increase and retain our life force, pranayama uses five tools:

- Locks or bandhas
- External retention or bahayia kumbhaka
- Internal retention or antar kumbhaka
- Exhalation rechaka
- Inhalation or poorak

When any exercise includes retentions along with locks, can we be able to speak about pranayama? Most of the breathing exercises people do are an easy version of pranayama. This can be accomplished by getting rid of the external retention and locks or holding your breath after exhaling.

Regular Breathing and Pranayama

Everyone knows how to breathe, even newborn babies. Nowadays, most people need to take a breathing class to help us deal with our daily lives, anxiety, tension, depression, driving, and work. Most people know that deep breathing could help overcome life's stresses, so we have to know the science behind breathing, pranayama.

Pranayama is an aspect of yoga that teaches us how to control and extend our breathing in several ways. It can teach us how to change the pattern, rate, and depth of our breathing.

Pranayama is being consciously aware of your breath. It is proper rhythmic, deep, and slow breathing. It can strengthen the respiratory system. It can soothe the nervous system. It can increase your concentration. Our breath connects our spirit, mind, and body.

Your breathing rate will change according to the circumstances around you like. It might increase because of a physical or emotional disturbance, but it will slow down when you are peaceful and calm. If you get tired when climbing a lot of stairs, you are going to get breathless. Try to do this to regulate your breathing so you won't feel as tired. While you are climbing the stairs, keep your shoulders straight. Breathe in deeply for two stairs, and then breathe out for two stairs. Continue a rhythm of two in and two out. By doing this, you will get rid of more carbon dioxide while taking in more oxygen, and you won't get as tired.

Most of the time, you only use a fraction of your lung capacity when you take shallow breaths. You aren't expanding your ribcage all the way. Your shoulders are usually hunched, and you have tension in your neck and upper back because we don't have enough oxygen in our bodies, which makes us tired and breathless. Try to keep your shoulder blades close together without straining and breathe out slowly and completely. You need to make sure you push all the air out of your lungs. Pause and then inhale in a gentle, slow, deep breath until your lungs are totally filled. Now breathe out through your nose without moving your shoulder blades. Continue doing this as many times as you can. When you do this, your brain is getting stimulated and will eliminate any tensions because you are giving your body a better oxygen supply.

Kinds of Breathing

Abdominal Breathing: these are deep abdominal breathing that will bring sir into the largest and lowest part of the lungs. Breathing will be deep and slow so that your diaphragm gets used properly.

Thoracic Breathing or Chest Breathing: you perform this breathing by contracting and expanding just the chest while you control your abdomen. This completely activates the middle part of the lungs.
Clavicular Breathing or Sectional Breathing: This is a shallow breathing technique where the abdomen is controlled, and you breathe by forcing air into the upper part of the lungs. Your collar bones and shoulders are raised while your stomach is being contracted when you inhale.

A complete pranayama breath will combine all of the above, starting with the stomach and consistently inhaling through the thoracic and onto the clavicular area. Your abdomen needs to expand out when you inhale and then contract when you exhale. In order to understand this motion better, sit down in a meditative posture; Vajrasana would be best, put your hands on your stomach. Breathe out slowly, and then breathe in through your nose. Move your hands away from each other when your stomach bulges. Now you will hold this breath for a second or two. Slowly breathe out, so your stomach retracts and brings your hands closer together. Hold this breath for a second or two and repeat this breathing cycle five times. You can use this ratio of breathing in for a count of four, hold for a count of two, breathe out for a count of eight, and hold for two. Your breathing needs to be rhythmic, slow, and deep.

The lower parts of your lungs will increase with the airflow. The rhythmic movements of your diaphragm will gently massage the stomach and will help your organs function better.

Pranayama needs to be done while sitting in a certain posture like Ardhpadmasana or Padmasana and needs to be done with an empty stomach and early in the mornings. Try your best to find a place that is well ventilated. Your breathing needs to be rhythmic and slow. Your eyes need to be closed so you can control your body and mind. You will be using the aspects of inhalation or poorka, retention or kumbhaka, and exhalation or rechaka.

Kinds of Pranayama:

- Kapalabhati Pranayama: this breathing will exhale air from your lungs a bit forcibly but will help you inhale involuntarily
- Bahya Pranayama: for this breath, you will breathe in forcibly, breathe out, and then hold your breath
- Shitali Pranayama: this is a cooling breath
- Bhastrika Pranayama: this breath forces the air in and out
- Brahamari Pranayama: this is the humming bee breath
- Anulom Vilom: this is an alternate breathing technique
- Ujjayi Pranayama: this is the victorious breath

Breath and Mind

The way you breathe can tell you about your current state of mind. You might be feeling good about yourself, you're thinking about having cocktails with some friends after work. You might be feeling stressed because you are trying to get everything in your "inbox" into your "outbox" before your day ends.

All stress isn't bad, but if you run on high-octane at all times, you could become a candidate for a massive burnout. Short-term stress could be great as it can help you reach that deadline. If you depend on short-term stress each day, you might find that your body gets worn out. Your immune system will get impacted, and your memory, attention, and mind will be impaired by long-term stress.

This is when your breathing comes into play. It can restore you. It can help you save energy for those moments in life when you need your mental resources.

Your breath can affect your mind and brain. You can learn a lot if you can learn to watch your breath and notice what is going on. Let's talk about our nose. Why do we have two nostrils? All we need is one large hole. There is a reason why we have two nostrils. If you breathe through the left nostril, it will engage the right side of the brain. If you breathe through the right nostril, it will engage the left side of the brain.
Researchers have found that when we breathe through the right nostril, our body's

metabolism engages twice as much as compared to breathing through the left nostril.

You know that when we were born, we inhaled deeply and began crying. The very last thing that we will do before we die is to take one last breath out, and then other people will begin crying. When you were born, you cried, but everyone else laughed. When you die, you will take on your last breath, and everyone else will cry. If that doesn't happen, you haven't lived your best life.

In our daily lives, we ignore our breath. There are four sources of energy:

- Calmness: this is a pleasant or happy state of mind
- Breath: this is the best source of energy. Our breathing could help us energize our entire system. If you're tired, try some deep breathing or change how you're breathing, you might just feel more energetic.
- Sleep: try not sleeping for just one night and see how well you feel the next morning.
- Food: fast for a few days, and you will realize what I'm talking about. If you eat

too much or too little, you are going to drain your energy

Just taking a few minutes and meditating will energize your system. Normally, people think that meditation is the same as concentration, but this isn't right. Meditation is the complete opposite of concentrating. Concentration is what you get after you meditate.

The Science Behind It

If you can observe things well, you can see a rhythm in nature; the seasons are a rhythm in nature. Our bodies have a rhythm, too. You might have noticed that you get hungry at the same times each day. You get sleepy at the same time; this is known as a biorhythm. No one can unlock your phone but you.
There is a rhythm in your breathing. It will be different during the morning, evening, and when you encounter various emotions. If you feel happy or smell your favorite flower, your breathing will be strong, steady, and slow, and your exhale will dissolve. If you feel angry or frustrated, your exhale will be a lot stronger.

There is a rhythm to your thought patterns and emotions. Your breathing will change with all the various emotions. It will be different when there is anger or fear. It all depends on how stressed you are, and there will be a rhythm in the changes within you.

Your breathing can bring harmony to these rhythms, and then life turns into music. It will take you three days and three hours to learn this. After you have learned this, you will only need to practice this for ten minutes each day. If you are a student and have an exam coming up, breathing can help you stay calm and enhance your intuition.

Does stress reduce longevity? Stress doesn't cause mortality, but it can affect us in various ways. If stress hormones increase, we are more susceptible to diseases and illnesses. You might be living, but you are going to be very sick. Relieving your stress is going to keep you healthy.

How can a person use breathing and meditation to handle pain or reduce all the negative impacts of stress? There have been millions of people who have gotten a handle on their depression by using breathing techniques. It can be used as an alternative to taking antidepressants.

Has there always been a connection between our minds and our breath? This connection is as old as the connection between our breath and our body. It goes back to the beginning of time.

This connection has been there in every ancient tradition. If you ever get the chance to watch the Maoris in New Zealand, they will greet one another by exchanging a breath. They will rub another person's nose, inhale, and exhale. This is the way they connect and make harmony between people.

Buddha told us just to observe our breath or Anapanasati. This can help you observe each sensation and goes beyond to see your true nature. Your breath doesn't have a religion or nationality. All of humankind need it.

Breath and Life

Ancient yogis saw that the breathing rate did correlate with how long we live and our health. They thought that to live to old age, a person had to breathe slowly. To show you this idea in more detail, we are going to talk about the animal kingdom. Humans do fall under primates such as apes and monkeys in the taxonomic order. We could train ourselves to breathe efficiently by practicing pranayama.

Never Pant Like Dogs

Among the vertebrates, the giant tortoise is probably the oldest living animal. Dogs breathe very fast and are on the total opposite side of the spectrum. They have a concise life span. Dogs will breathe 20 to 30 times each minute and live between ten and 20 years.

The giant tortoise only breathes four times each minute and can live to be 150 years old. The oldest living tortoise was thought to be over 250 years old. A tortoise named "Jonathan" is at 186 years right now and is the oldest living animal known to man. From this point on, if you see that you are breathing fast, try to take some slower breaths.

Breathe Consciously, Breathe Slow

We take breathing for granted because it is one of the many things that we do automatically, such as our heart beating or our body temperature staying the same. This is all controlled by our nervous system, and our breath isn't anything that you have to be aware of every minute of every day. Used correctly, it could help change your state. Your breath is a tool that works on both your mind and body.

Having a slower breathing rate can positively affect your mood. It turns off the chemicals that are created by responding to stress. It can increase the immune system in your body. Anytime you get stressed, you will normally have shallow breaths coming from your chest. This can cause a lot of harm over the years. If our stress becomes chronic, we have to take control to keep away illnesses and pain. If you have control over your breathing, you have found the key to your mental and physical health.

Even if you are working out or just running, it is best to keep your mind calm and your tongue in your mouth. Focusing on breathing in through your nose and out through your mouth is the best way to handle more demanding and longer tasks.

If you just breathe in and out through your mouth, it will tap into your sympathetic nervous system and trigger your flight or fight response. This might work if you have to run a sprint, and you need to move as fast as possible, but mouth breathing can deplete your body's responses.

Slow Breathing Is Healthy

An average human will breathe between 12 to 18 times each minute. This is what every first aid book will tell you. Breathing about 12 times is fine, but when you hit 16, your body is experiencing some stress.

With more advanced yogis and healthy, active people, a normal breath rate might be a lot lower, contributing to a long life. A lower breath rate will reduce the heart's stress and keep it going for many, many years. When you add some physical activities while breathing, it can stretch your body's ability to handle stress. The body's stress response does have its limits. When it has to stop, there is a point that turns off the hormones that can help you handle your stress triggers. Your body is going to need some time to recover.

Pranayama Terminology

There are many different words that you have come across already and will come across throughout this book. To ensure that you fully understand what they all mean, we will go over a few important words that you need to know.

Ajapa – Ajapa is a type of meditation technique that places focus on the natural sound of your breath. This meditation practice is considered a form of yoga. Broken down, the word comes from "a," meaning "not," and "japa," meaning "repeated." That means the word means "not repeated." Within the context of this yoga, japa refers to the effortful repetition of the sound. That means ajapa is the effortless repeated sound, like a person's natural breath. With enough practice, control your breath's sound through this yoga is believed to create feelings of kindness, compassion, and peace.

Anasakti Yoga – Anasakti yoga is a way of life and philosophy advocated by Mahatma Gandhi. It encourages people not to create an attachment to the material world. Anasakti yoga teaches you how to let go of attachments as a result of a person's actions. It is believed that non-attachment will help liberate people from suffering. The practitioner won't be bound by attachment to the material world, thus helping them find eternal life. Those who practice this form of yoga is still fully dedicated to and engaged in their work and actions, but they don't have any attachment to the outcome.

Apana – Apana is the second most crucial vayus or types of prana within Hatha yoga. Vayu, in Sanskrit, means "wind" and refers to how prana moves through the body. Apana vayu regulates your prana's outward flow and is in control of the elimination of physical wastes and toxins. This is located within the pelvic floor and spread up to the lower abdomen, regulating reproductive functions and digestion.

Arhatic Yoga – Arhatic yoga is a system for spiritual growth created to help people evolve their souls faster to serve humankind and the Earth. This yoga process involves breathing techniques, meditation, asanas, and spiritual practices that are brought together into a single cohesive system.

Ashtanga – Ashtanga yoga is a very physical form of yoga created by T. Krishnamacharya and Sri K. Pattabhi Jois. It was derived from Hatha yoga. Ashtanga means "eight limbs" and refers to the eight-fold path or eight yoga limbs outlined in the *Yoga Sutras*. It is a dynamic, flowing style that will connect the body and the breath. This method stresses the fact you have to practice every day.

Bhastrika – Bhastrika is bellows breath and is a type of pranayama. It is considered one of the most important breathing techniques. It is derived from the Sanskrit word for "bellows" because of how the abdomen pumps the breath. It requires you to take rapid and powerful inhales and exhales, which will make an audible sound. It can help cleanse the airways and increase the energy of the mind and body.

Bindi – Bindi is a mark of protection that many Hindus wear in the center of their forehead. It comes from the word Bindu, meaning dot or point. Bindu refers to the point where creation began, and the bindi they wear symbolizes that. Traditionally, the bindi is white, red, or yellow.

Desa – Desa originates from a Sanskrit word that translates to country, place, or space. In traditional Indian culture, desa is the same as the county. It is a geo-cultural unit. Within yoga, desa is the location in the body, particularly when it comes to breathing exercises. Desa is also a way to treat imbalances or diseases in the body within Ayurveda.

Egoism – Egoism is a behavior display that is motivated by a person's self-interest. It also refers to the idea that self-interest is the basis of all moral behavior.

Hasta Vinyasa – Hasta vinyasa is a sequence of movements in yoga that involves arm movements. It comes from hasta, meaning "formed with the hands," and vinyasa, meaning "coordinated movement."

Hatha Yoga – *Hatha Yoga Pradipika* was written in the 15th century by Swami Svatmarama. It is the oldest surviving manual of Hatha yoga and is considered one of the three most important yoga texts. Hatha yoga is meant to lead the practitioner through the awareness of their body to the Self's awareness. It is made up of asanas, pranayama, mudras, bandhas, and Samadhi.

Kosha – Koshas are considered the five layers of awareness that veil the true self. To discover each layer helps to bring you closer to oneness with the true self and universe. Kash means "covering" or "sheath." That's why the koshas are often called the five sheaths. Practicing yoga will take a person deeper into the self through the koshas.

Kripalu Yoga – Kripalu Yoga is a modern yoga style that was adapted from ancient Hatha practices. It is made up of sequences of asanas in no certain order and relaxation and breathing exercises. This yoga aims to help guide your awareness inward to focus on the flow of prana.

Kundalini – Kundalini means "coiled one." It refers to a primal force that lives "coiled" at the base of your spine. Different yoga poses, meditation, and controlled breathing can help awaken the kundalini and enlighten your chakras.

Manipura – Manipura is the name for the solar plexus chakra. Mani translates to "gem," while Pura means "city." That literal translates the word to the "city of jewels." That helps us to think of this chakra as our personal treasure and center of wellbeing.

Mudra – Murda is a type of symbolic and sacred gesture that is found in yoga. One of the most well-known mudras is used during meditation and yoga practices to help channel the flow of prana. It translates to seal, gesture, or mark. Across different traditions and religions, there are around 400 mudras. Each one has a unique symbolism and is believed to have a specific effect on the mind and body.

Nadi – Nadi translates to flow, tube, or channel. It is the network of channels through which your energy travels. The number of nadis that a person has depends on the tradition, but there seem to be three principal nadis that move throughout the spinal cord and chakras.

Pavan – Pavana means air and is one of the five elements of the universe. In the Hindu belief, these five elements will dissolve upon death. The other elements are Aakash (sky), Agni (fire), Jala (water), and bhumi (earth).

Pingala – Pingala is one of the nadis of the astral body. It is located from the right nostril and runs down to the root chakra. It runs along the right side of the spinal cord. It is objective, rational, analytical, and can be aggressive.

Prana – Prana is a Sanskrit word with several English translations, including vital principle, energy, and life force. It refers to all of the manifesting energy in the universe and is present in living things and inanimate objects.

Rasa – Rasa means fluid, sap, or essence. Spiritually, it refers to the essence of human experience. It is the emotions that govern our life. Tantric beliefs have nine basic human emotions. Within yoga, only three of the rasas are thought to be fundamental.

Samadhi – This is the final step along the path of yoga. It translates to liberation, bliss, and enlightenment. In Buddhism and

Hinduism, it is seen as the pinnacle of all intellectual and spiritual activity.

Shodhana – This Sanskrit word means purifying or cleaning. It is often paired with Nadi. Nadi shodhana is a calming breathing exercise that helps to relieve tension, stress, and fatigue.

Sitali – This Sanskrit word translates to soothing or cooling. It is usually used to describe a form of pranayama. With sitali, the tongue will be rolled, and the breath is pulled in through the tongue as if you were breathing through a straw.

Tantra Yoga – Tantra is a type of yoga that uses different rituals to learn about the universe through the human microcosm. It seeks to balance out human instincts to reach enlightenment.

Tapasya – Tapasya literal means "generation of heat and energy." It involves self-discipline, moderation, deep meditation, and efforts to find Self-realization. Gurus and monks in Hinduism, Jainism, and Buddhism practice this to reach spiritual liberation.

Yogini – This refers to a female yoga master. Its male counterpart is yogi. It translates to the enlightened goddess.

Yuj – Yuj means to join. The word yoga comes from, which is a spiritual, physical, and mental practice that originated in ancient India. Yuj is yoga's root word, which is that yoga looks to unite the spirit, body, and mind.

Precautions

There are some precautions that you need to take before you begin practicing pranayama:

- You should never practice pranayama if your lungs are congested.

- Make sure you do pranayama in a room that is well ventilated, or practice it outside.

- You should never practice pranayama in a hurry.

- If you regularly practice pranayama and asanas, do your asanas before you do pranayama. After you practice your asanas, relax in a Shavasana pose before you do your pranayama. Don't do anything strenuous after you have done your pranayama.

- Never practice pranayama if you feel tired. Try to relax for 15 minutes in the Shavasana pose before doing your pranayama.

- If you are feeling any discomfort or tiredness, stop the pranayama. Lie down in the Shavasana while breathing normally. Talk to a yoga specialist before beginning your pranayama.

- If you are a beginner at pranayama, you shouldn't hold your breath. Once you have become comfortable with the pranayama basics, you can learn to hold your breath while being guided by an expert after mastering yoga breathing basics.

- It would help if you did not practice pranayama right after you have eaten. You will need to wait about three hours after you eat. Heavy meals are going to take a lot longer to digest. If you do your pranayama during the evening, eat a healthy snack that can be digested by the time you begin your pranayama.

- Don't make any loud sounds during your breathing. Make sure your breathing stays steady and rhythmic.

- You should never strain during your pranayama practice. Your lungs are very delicate. Make sure your breathing isn't forced beyond its limits.

- Always breathe through your nose unless you are told not to do so.

- Pranayama needs to be practiced after you have gained control over your body by mastering all the asanas. Practicing pranayama will generate energy within your body, while yoga asanas eliminate the blockages that keep the body's energy flowing.

- If you have any chronic medical conditions, ask your yoga teacher and doctor before your start pranayama.

- If you have a hernia, high blood pressure, or heart disease, you should never do bhastrika or Kapal Bhati pranayama. If you are doing kapalabhati and are a beginner, make sure you exhale very gently and never use excessive force.

- If you have low blood pressure, never do skitkari pranayama. Never do this pranayama during the winter months.

- Never do suryabhedi during the summer months.

- Never do chandrabhedi during the winter months.

- Those who have a hernia or high blood pressure should not practice agnisar pranayama. Never do this pranayama after you have had surgery on your stomach.

Chapter 2: The Importance of Correct Breath

I mentioned in the introduction that humans don't breathe correctly. However, unless we are physically out of breath, most of us don't think about how we breathe. This is why many of us are breathing incorrectly and use only about a third of our lungs. Studies have found that this could be the cause of several health issues. When we don't breathe fully, it leaves us feeling drained, depressed, anxious, stressed and affects our sleep.

In a single day, we breathe about 20,000 times. It helps the immune, cardiovascular, digestive, muscular, and nervous systems. Around 70% of the toxins in our body leave through our breath. The lungs' main function is to move the oxygen within the air we breathe to enter our red blood cells. The red blood cells then carry the oxygen throughout the body. The lungs also help to remove CO_2 when we exhale.

There are several breathing mistakes that people make that constrict lung capacity. These include:

- Unconsciously holding the breath
  Signs of holding your breath can be sighing more than usual, which is your body's way of getting extra oxygen, especially when you are anxious or stress. You will likely be a chest breath and feel a tightness in your shoulders and neck.

- Breathing through your mouth
  Breathing through the mouth instead of the nose is a very common habit that can cause you to feel tired and give you a dry mouth. When you don't breathe well through your nose, it can alter your blood pressure and heart rate. It also increases your stress response. Nitric oxide is also produced in the nose, which, once inhales, significantly improves their ability to absorb oxygen. This is extremely important when you are exercising.

To help you figure out if you are breathing properly or not, the following are four signs of improper breathing. After that, you will find six tests you can do to see if you are breathing improperly.

The first sign of bad breathing is often yawning. Yawning is usually triggered when you are tired, but it can also be triggered by shortness of breath or shallow breathing. This is especially true if you are overweight or if you have health problems.

The second sign is that you grind your teeth while you are sleeping. When you breathe incorrectly, it is often accompanied by tooth grinding because both of these are common symptoms of stress.

The third sign is that you have a tightness in your shoulders and neck. Around 80% of us are upper chest breathers. Instead of taking deep breaths, we take shallow breaths, which causes the muscles within the back, shoulders, and neck to overcompensate, and will tighten up to help the body breathe deeper so that the lungs can get more air.

The fourth sign is that you always feel tired. The most common side effect of incorrect breathing is that you feel tired because you can't access enough of the respiratory system.

With that in mind, let's try these tests for improper breathing.

1. Upper-Chest Breathing
   You will lie on your back and place one of your hands on your upper chest and the other on your belly for this test. Lie here for a few minutes and notice how your hands move. If the hand on your chest moves when you breathe, but the one on your belly doesn't, then you are a chest-breather. Anything more than a slight movement from your chest shows that you may not be breathing efficiently.

2. Shallow Breathing
   Again, you will lie on your back for this test and place your hands around your lower ribs, one hand on either side. As you breathe, you should feel an effortless expansion of the ribs as you take a breath in and a slow recoil as you release the breath. If the ribs don't move, then your breath is too shallow, even if you can see your belly moving.

3. Overbreathing
   While you're still lying down, take a few minutes to allow your body to establish a relaxed breathing rate. Then begin to count the length of your next exhale and then compare it to how long the next

inhale is. You want your exhale to be a bit longer. If it isn't, then you are an over breather. For a second test, try to short how long your inhale takes. If this causes any type of distress, you are likely an over breather. Since it is easy to manipulate how these tests turn out, you may want to ask somebody else to count for you at a time when you aren't paying attention.

4. Breath Holding
   Holding your breath after you take an inhale is likely one of the most common poor breathing habits. To figure out if you do this, focus on the transition between inhale and exhale. A breath-holder will mostly likely feel a "catch" and might notice that they struggle to start the exhale. This tends to be more noticeable when you exercise. This can be reduced by consciously relaxing the belly right when the inhale ends.

5. Reverse Breathing
   A reverse breath happens when the diaphragm gets pulled into the chest when you inhale and drops when you exhale. Lay down and put a hand on

your abdomen. Your belly should slowly flatten when your breath out and rise when you breathe in. If the opposite happens, then you are a reverse breather. Since this type of breathing is more likely to happen when you are exerting yourself, it isn't completely reliable.

6. Mouth Breathing
   It is pretty easy to tell if you are a mouth breather. If you aren't completely sure, all you need to do is ask a friend or catch yourself when you aren't focusing on your breath.

Those exercises serve a purpose. You must realize how you breathe; that way, you can actively fix that. This is so important because breathing has a bigger impact on our health than we think. Breathing is so important that humankind long ago noted how valuable it is to survival and how the body and mind function.

As early as the first millennium BCE, the religions Tao and Hinduism placed extreme importance on a "vital principle" that flows through us, a type of energy, and viewed breathing as a form of its manifestation. In

Tao, this is referred to as qi, and the Hindus call it prana, as we have learned.

Sometime later, the Greek term pneuma and ruah in Hebrew referred to the divine presence and breath. In Latin based languages, spiritus is at the root of respiration and spirit. Pranayama was the first form of breath retention to build on the theory around controlling the respiratory system to help increase longevity.

Johannes Heinrich Schultz, a German psychiatrist, created "autogenic training" in the 1920s to help people relax. This approach was based upon a slow and deep breath and is likely one of the West's most well-known breathing techniques. Several contemporary forms of mindfulness meditation emphasize breathing-based exercises.

Every meditation, relaxation, or calming technique relies on the breath, which could be the lowest common denominator in every approach to calm the mind and body. Research into physiology and the effects of breath-control provides credence to the value of regulating and monitoring our breathing. Even if you only have a basic understanding of physiology helps explain controlled breath induces relaxation. We all know that emotions affect our bodies. When we are happy, the corners of the mouth will turn up, and the edges of the eyes will crinkle into a characteristic expression.

The autonomic nervous system, ANS, connects the brain to the body through a two-way street. If you are experiencing nervousness or anxiety about things happening in your life, the brain will switch on the sympathetic nervous system via the nerves of the ANS. This is what is known as our fight or flight response. This will cause your heart to beat faster and your breath to increase, among other things.
Similarly, if you are safe and calm, at rest, or engaged in something you find pleasant, the breath will deepen and slow. This is when you are under the influence of your parasympathetic nervous system, which creates a relaxing effect. What is less known is that the effects happen in the opposite direction. The state of the body will affect the emotions. Studies have found that when your face smiles, the brain will respond in kind. This means you will start to experience more pleasant emotions. Breathing has the same type of effect.

The heart and lungs can give our brains feedback and tell them that things are fine, even if they aren't. One interesting way this happens involves the relationship our lungs and heart has and their nerves. Every time you breathe in, the heart is told to beat a bit faster. When you exhale, the heart slows down a bit. The overall effect is that there is a slight change in your heart rate every minute.

But if you take the time to make one part of this cycle longer than the other and do this for a few minutes, the accumulated effect will either increase or decrease your heart rate. If the inhales stay longer for a few minutes, your heart rate will increase. This is because it sends a message to the brain that things should be a bit more active in the body and brain, stimulating the sympathetic nervous system. The opposite is true when you make the exhales longer. The parasympathetic nervous system gets triggered, and the body tells the brain that things are good and slow down the body.

This is very evident in people who have breathing problems. When these difficulties tend to be acute or sporadic, it can trigger a panic attack. If they are chronic, they often induce a muted anxiety. It is estimated that around 60% of people with COPD have depressive disorders or anxiety. These disorders likely stem from concerns about what the disease may end up doing to them, but purely mechanical factors also contribute to this. The difficulty that they experience often leads to faster breathing, which doesn't have with their oxygen supply but will aggravate their anxiety and physical discomfort.

Rapid breathing has the power to exacerbate and contribute to panic attacks through the cycle of fear triggering a faster breath, which then increases fear. Georg Alpers, in 2005, along with the help of his colleagues, observed significant and unconscious hyperventilation when a person with a driving phobia headed out on the highway.

Whether or not the anxiety is caused by breathing issues or other issues, it can be eased through a number of breathing techniques derived from Eastern approaches. For example, follow your breath is a technique that turns the attention to the breath and is one of the first parts of mindfulness meditation. When you combine reassuring thoughts with the breath, you can control your nervous system.

Research has found that the vagus nerve and certain chemical neurotransmitters are the reasons for the effects that a change in breathing has on the heart rate. Remember that the ANS is just trying to keep your background systems balanced and working correctly to the day's ever-changing circumstances.

Nadi and Svara

Svara is a breathing technique that helps you control your breath by alternating the breathing cycles through the right and left nostrils. This goal of this is to help balance the flow of your prana through your energy channels, nadis, so that you can reach spiritual, physical, and mental health.

Svara is Sanskrit, meaning tone or sound. There are two main nadis. The ida and Pingala and represent the airflow through the right and left nostrils. Yogis have found that through this physical connection of ida and Pingala, you can influence the vital and mental energies in the body to awaken sushumna. This was when they came up with the various techniques to balance the svara. There are many techniques to balance the svara, but the main one is nadi shodhana pranayama, which means to purify the fine energy network of the nadi in the body.

This is what has become known as alternate nostril breathing.

With this pranayam, you establish a breathing pattern through the right and left nostrils and focus on how the air flows through your nostrils. There are various stages of this from simple to sophisticated, but the essence remains; this breathing pattern balance purifies and tones the energies within the mind and body. There are also more specific pranayamas, such as surya bheda, where the Pingala is stimulated when you breathe only through the right nostril. Chandra bheda when the ida is stimulated by breathing through the left nostril only.

Diaphragmatic Breathing

Diaphragmatic breathing is a specific breathing practice that requires you to take a deep that fully engages the diaphragm. The diaphragm is a dome-shaped muscle located underneath the lungs and controls your respiratory function. When taking a breath in, your diaphragm is pushed downwards. This simple movement will form a series of events. Next, your lungs will start to expand, which will cause negative pressure, drawing air in through your mouth and nose. After you start to release the breath, your diaphragm will push up, which will help to push all of the air from your lungs.

Stress, poor postures, restrictive clothing, and conditions that weaken your breathing muscles can cause a person to become a chest breather. Some research suggests that diaphragmatic breathing can help those who have COPD. Diaphragmatic breathing means that you are fully engaging your stomach, diaphragm, and abdominal muscles when you breathe.

Since you're here, you probably want to know how to perform diaphragmatic breathing. This simple technique can give you a good foundation of what to expect in the pranayama breathing techniques.

Come into a comfortable seated position, or lie down. If you decide to sit in a chair, make sure that you have your feet flat on the floor and that your head, shoulders, and neck are relaxed. You don't want to keep your back stick straight to the point where you are uncomfortable, and you also shouldn't be slouching. If you are lying down, place a pillow under the head and knees to be more comfortable. You can also bend your knees if you would like.

Place one of your hands on your upper chest. When you are breathing and properly engaging your diaphragm, this hand should stay still as you are breathing. Place your other hand under your ribcage. The epigastric area you are feeling will help you feel the diaphragm as you are breathing.

Take a slow breath in through your nose. You want the air moving in through your nose to make its way down into the lungs so that the belly rises. Make sure that you don't force or push your ab muscles out. You want the airflow and movement to be smooth. This should only use this epigastric area. You shouldn't feel as if you have to force the low-abdomen out by squeezing the muscles. You also shouldn't feel the hand on your chest move that much.

Release the breath through your mouth and allow your belly to relax. Your hand on your belly should fall inward. Don't try to force your stomach in by clenching or squeezing these muscles. Make sure you breathe out slowly and through slightly pursed lips. Again, the hand resting on your chest should remain virtually still.

If you find that this feels awkward at first, it is probably because you are used to breathing with your chest. While the frequency in which you do this will vary depending on your health, it is typically done three times at first. The majority of people will choose to do it for five to ten minutes, one to four times each day. If at any point you notice that you feel dizzy or lightheaded, stop this breathing exercise and lay down if you aren't already. This is considered to be a natural way to breathe.

Since diaphragmatic breathing helps you engage the diaphragm, it can provide you with several benefits, including:

- Promote relaxation
- Reduce oxygen demand
- Lower the blood pressure and heart rate
- Improve core muscle stability
- Strengthen the diaphragm

While diaphragmatic breathing has been known to help people with asthma and COPD, it should not be used as a standalone treatment. It can also help with anxiety, but if done incorrectly, it can worsen the symptoms. People with respiratory conditions need to be careful when they first start practicing this type of breathing. It can start out causing increased fatigue and labored breathing. It would help if

you built up this practice gradually to see the benefits.

Breathing Postures

When you practice the next chapter's pranayama techniques, you will need to know what posture you will use. There are several different yoga poses you can choose from. We'll go over some of the most common poses that you can use when practicing pranayama.

Easy Pose (sukhasana)

Easy pose is the best pose for the beginner or anybody who hasn't practice yoga. It's called easy pose for a reason. Easy pose is a simple cross-legged seated position—it what most grade-school children sit in during circle time.

Sit on the ground or your mat with your legs out in front of you and your back straight to get into this position. Slowly fold the right foot under your left thigh and then the left foot under your right thigh. Your legs should cross at mid-shins and not at the ankles. Shift your buttocks so that you are on your sit-bones and make sure that your spine is in alignment. You can also place a pillow or bolster under your buttocks to lift your hips if you are experiencing any discomfort.

This tends to be a good pose for anybody, but if you have knee problems, such as arthritis or knee surgery, this position may not be the best. Also, if you have a backache, you may not be able to stay in this position for longer than five minutes.

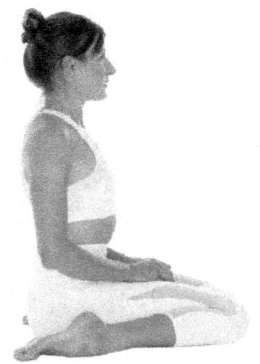

Hero Pose (virasana)

This is a little more advance than an easy pose, and it probably not the best option for beginners.

To get into this pose, start by kneeling on the floor. You can place a bolster or folded blanket between your thighs and calves if you need to. Make sure your thighs are perpendicular to the floor and bring your inner knees together. Slide your feet out so that they are slightly wider than your hips. The tops of your feet should be against the floor.

Exhale and then move back halfway. Your torso should be leaned slightly forward. Place your thumbs into the bend of your knees, and pull the skin of your calf muscles towards the heels. Then you should sit down between the space between your feet.

If you find that your buttocks don't rest comfortably on the floor, raise them on a thick book or block placed between your feet. Your sitting bones need to be evenly supported. You should have thumb's-width space between your heels and outer hips. Turn the thighs in and push the top of the thigh bones into the floor. Place your hands in your lap.

Lift your sternum and roll your shoulders up and down the back. Lengthen your tailbone into the floor so that you are anchored into the torso.

This pose should be used with caution by those who have heart problems or headaches also if you have ankle or knee injuries. If you do, you should avoid this pose unless you have some assistance from an instructor.

Thunderbolt Pose (Vajrayana)

This is an ancient and traditional seated pose and is similar to the hero pose that we just did. You can move into this pose the same as the hero pose, but the only thing that you won't do is separate your feet. Your heels should remain touching, and your buttocks will rest on top of them.

Start by kneeling with your buttocks and hips lifted off of your legs. If you need some extra padding, place a blanket under your feet, shins, and knees. Your thighs need to be perpendicular to the floor, and your inner knees should be together.

Un-tuck the toes and keep your feet firmly pressed into the floor. With an exhale, come to rest on your heels. Your feet and shins should be in line, and your feet should not splay open or turn in.

Keep your back straight and bring your shoulders up and back down your back to relax. Keep your collarbones wide and lengthen your tailbone towards the floor.

Like the hero pose, this should be avoided if you have a recent or current ankle or knee injury.

Half Lotus Pose (Ardha padmasana)

Everybody thinks about the lotus pose when it comes to seated yoga poses, but it is more advance and a pose that some people can't do. A good option is to do the half lotus pose. While it is easier than the lotus pose, it can still be too difficult for absolute beginners.

To get into this position, start by sitting on the floor with your legs straight out in front of you and your spine straight.

Bend your right knee and hug it to your chest. Then take your right ankle over to the crease of your left hip so that the bottom of your foot is pointed towards the sky. The top of the foot should be against the hip crease.

Bend the left knee and then bring the left ankle under the right knee.

Make sure that your spine stays straight, and your shoulders are relaxed.

This pose should be avoided if you have any recent hip, ankle, or knee injuries. If your ankles, knees, or hips are tight, you could find it hard to cross your legs. Don't force yourself into this pose.

Lotus Pose (padmasana)

To get into this pose, start seated on the floor with your legs extended in front of you and your back straight.

Bend your right knee and externally rotate your hip so that your knee falls to the right. Bring your right ankle into your left hand and the knee in your right hand. Bring your foot to rest on the crease of your left leg, pressing the top of your foot into the hip crease. Bring the right knee to rest on the floor.

Lean back and then start to bend your left knee, and draw the left foot towards your right knee. Hold the left ankle in your right hand and carefully bring your left heel into your right hip crease.

Keep your back straight, and your shoulders relaxed.

This pose should not be used by beginners or anything with ankle, knee, or hip problems. Don't force your legs into this position. It is best to move slowly and mindfully and stop if you experience any type of pain.

Auspicious Pose (swastikasana)

This is a relatively easy post to get into and can be held for prolonged periods. Some people find this easier to do than easy pose.

To get into this position, start by sitting on the floor with your legs out in front of you. Start by folding your left leg in and place the left leg's sole against your inner thigh of the opposite leg.

Bend your right leg and place your right foot in the area between the calf and left thigh muscles. Hold your left foot by the toes, carefully pull it up, and put it between the right thigh and calf.

Make sure that your knees are touching the floor.

This pose should be avoided by people who have sacral infections or issues with sciatica to pinch the nerve.

Accomplished Pose (siddhasana)

This is another simple beginner pose. To get into the pose, start by sitting on the floor and cross your legs. Place one foot close to the inner thigh and then bring the other foot close into the ankle so that both of the heels are nearly at the midline.

Make sure that your back is straight and your shoulders are relaxed. If you need to, you can place a blanket under your hip bones or knees.

Like with easy pose and auspicious pose, be careful if you have sciatica, knee, or hip problems.

Picking Your Best Pose

You must pick out the best pose for you and what your body can do. Never force yourself into a pose, as this is only going to cause more problems. If the poses we have gone over does not work for you, you can always sit in a chair, making sure your back does not rest against the back of the chair.

If you do have healthy hips and ankles, then you can try any of the above poses. The most commonly used pose would be easy pose. The most important thing is that you remember that to have a sustainable, healthy, and energizing experience, you choose a position that will allow you to be comfortable.

Chapter 3: Pranayama Breath

Before you begin your practice of pranayama breathing, you must understand the basic guidelines of this practice. Let's going over some of these guidelines so that you are prepared.

1. It doesn't hurt to do some stretches to warm up the body and get the breath flowing.

2. Always breathe through the nose unless told to do otherwise or if you have a breathing obstruction. When you breathe, your abdomen should expand on the inhale. The chest should only move slightly with your breath.

3. Make sure that your face, nose, and mouth are relaxed.

4. Don't force your breath or retentions to last longer than what is comfortable. If you try to force it, then it will only agitate your mind.

5. It works better if both of your nostrils are equally open. If one side seems to be

closed, try lying on the opposite side of your body for 30 to 60 seconds.

6. Make sure you listen to your limits. You can overdo simple pranayama. It could be that it's not the right technique for you. If you start feeling off-center, spacey, irritable, agitated, or anxious, stop, and return to your regular breath.

With that in mind, what constitutes a full yogic breath cycle? Let's find out. A full yogic breath will start with deep and fluid inhalations that will fill three areas of your torso independently. First, you fill the lower abdomen. Then, the mid-section of the torso will be filled with breath, expanding the ribs and diaphragm. Lastly, the breath will fill the upper chest and shoulders just as the inhale comes to an end. This purposeful and slow inhale will be followed by a long, slow exhale, releasing the breath from those three sections in reverse order. The complete round of yogic breath will include one complete inhale, and one complete exhale.

You want to make sure that both the inhale and exhale are fluid and continuous. At no point should you ever feel any type of strain. Remember that it can take some time to develop a relaxed relationship with pranayama, especially if you have never done it before. This is why pranayama is considered a practice. What is more important is that you set the intention to develop your capacity for breathing intentionally, fluidly, and without struggle or tension.

To practice full yogic breath, do the following:

1. Pick a comfortable seated position. Ensure that your pelvic bones are rooted into the floor under you and that your spine is straight. You can also lie down if you prefer.

2. Close your eyes and take a moment to settle in. Close your mouth, and breath through the nostrils. Let the mind quiet and focus on the natural flow of breath. Live in the present.

3. Once ready, inhale slowly and with purpose. Draw the breath deep in the low abdomen, beginning at the pelvic floor, and slowly let the breath fill up to the navel and then out and away from the spine. Focus, first, on filling the lower abdomen.

4. As you fill this area with the breath, let it expand in every direction as it moves up towards the navel.

5. Once this space is filled, continue inhaling to fill the mid-torso. Continue drawing the breath up, from the navel to the ribs, and let the breath gently expand the diaphragm, ribs, and mid-back.

6. Once you have filled the mid-torso with the breath, complete your inhale by drawing the breath into the upper chest, filling the sternum and heart, and then the shoulders and the base of the neck. Feel your collarbones lift a bit.

7. Allow the natural pause that may occur at the top of your breath to happen. The surrender to the long, slow exhale. Release the breath from the upper chest, down to the mid-torso, and emptying the lower abdomen. Feel the belly contract and draw in.

8. Your exhale may be followed by a natural pause. Let this happen before starting the next round.

Practice this for several rounds, upwards of 15 minutes, and then allow your breath to return to normal before opening your eyes.

Preparing

Before you start any pranayama practice, you have to get yourself ready. The first thing you need to look at is the time of day you intend to practice. Typically, pranayama is practiced early in the morning. This is the time of day when the body is rested, and the mind is calm. However, to wake up earlier than you will require you to go to bed earlier. You also have to get rid of distractions like television and other technology to promote rest. Don't worry, though; if mornings are right for you, cooling practices like ujjayi, Nadi shodhana, and dirgha can be done before you go to bed.

Consistency is much more important than the duration. Ensure that you pick the most realistic time for you to practice. Even if you can only practice for ten to 15 minutes, as long as you can do it each day, that's all that matters. It is best if you do your pranayama at the same each day. Doing it simultaneously and in the same place will help cultivate the discipline to keep doing it.

Speaking of place, you must practice pranayama in a well-ventilated room. Try to avoid practicing under a fan or close to an air conditioner, as this can be distracting and can give you a chill. You should try to keep this area uncluttered. Make this space sacred to your, clean, and safe. If you can, you can practice outside if the weather allows, and you don't suffer from allergies that could hamper your practice.

Next, make sure that you haven't eaten anything for three to four hours before your practice. This is why practicing first thing in the morning is best. It is hard to perform breathing techniques when you have a full stomach. The food you eat, how much you ate, and how late you ate the night before is going to impact your pranayama the next morning.

Then, you need to make sure you get rid of all distractions. You have to turn off your phones, don't just switch them to vibrate, and put them away. You also need to turn off and put away computers and tablets to get interrupted. If you have friends or neighbors the drop-in or regularly call, inform them of what you are doing not to interrupt you.

If you are menstruating, practices like nadi shodhana, dirgha, and ujjayi can help alleviate cramps and other symptoms while lessening fatigue. If you are pregnant, speak with your doctor and think about joining a prenatal yoga class.

Right before your practice, you can perform a nasal wash. A neti pot is probably the easiest way to do this.

It's very easy not to be consistent with your practice. These guidelines let you know how you can get started and what could cause you to stop practicing. Please use the information to help you ensure you're prepared to help avoid possible pitfalls before they occur.

Purifying of Nadis

Within the body, 72,000 nadis move prana to various areas of the body. However, impurities can cause some of the nadis to stop working. First, you have to activate the Nadi, and then you can purify them to carry prana efficiently again.

Pingala and Ida nadis can be activated through voluntary breathing methods, like pranayama. When you purposefully breathe in and out with only the right nostril, it will activate the Pingala

Nadi. When you breathe in and out with only the left nostril, it activates the Ida nadi.

To awaken Sushmna, you have to find equilibrium with these two nadis. Once you reach a balance between these nadis, it can help facilitate a Kundalini awakening. If you don't reach a balance, Sushumna will remain closed, and Kundalini will remain dormant. Pingala and Ida's equilibrium is possible only after small nadis, known as Nadikas, attached to these two main nadis get purified somehow.

It is important that your practice Nadi Shuddhi Pranayama before yoga to help cleanse the nadis. If impurities block the nadis, prana shakti can't move through your nadis. Nadi purification can be done in two ways:

1. Smanu – this is a mental process that requires you to say the Bija mantra
2. Nirmanu – this is a physical cleansing of Shatkarmas, like Dhauti kriya.

Samanu is an advanced practice that will flush out the impurities. A samanu practice is normally done sitting in lotus pose, but if you can't comfortably get into that pose, choose any of the others we went over earlier. As you perform this, you will be saying the vayu bija mantra in your head over and over again. The mantra is "yam." This is an advanced practice, so this might not be something you should do if you are new to pranayam, yoga, and other such practices, so proceed with caution.

1. Holding the right nostril close, breathe in through the left nostril while mentally saying "yam" 16 times.
2. Hold your breath at the time and mentally say "yam" for another 64 times.
3. Close the left nostril, and breathe out through your right nostril while mentally saying "yam" 32 times.

Then you will move to use the Agni bija mantra. This is going to take the Agni tattva, the fire element, and joint it with the Prithvi tattva, the earth element. The agni bija mantra is "ram."

1. Holding the left nostril close, breathe in through the left nostril and mentally chant "ram" 16 times.
2. Hold the breath and mentally chant "ram" 64 times
3. Hold the right nostril close, and release your breath through the left while mentally chanting "ram" 32 times.

Move your gaze to the tip of your nose and think about the luminous reflection of the moon as you mentally chant the bija mantra "tham."

1. Hold the right nostril and breathe in through the left nostril while mentally chanting "tham" 16 times.
2. Hold the breath and mentally chant "tham" 64 times.
3. Hold the left nostril and release the breath through the right nostril while mentally chanting "tham" 32 times.

Once you have practiced these three pranayamas, your nadis will be purified. Again, if you find this too hard to do, that's okay. You can work up to it.

Bhastrika

When you start feeling sluggish, don't reach for that fifth cup of coffee; try doing this breathing exercise. Bhastrika, or "bellows breath," helps to increase your flow of prana. Most people use this to help energize their body and to help calm an overactive mind. Whenever you start feeling hazy or trudging through mud, Bhastrika can help clear the fog. It is considered a heating breathing practice that mimics fanning a fire.

The name describes the active filling and emptying of the lungs and stomach during the practice. It helps to stoke the inner fire of your body and mind, supporting your digestion. It can help balance the Vata and Kapha, but your should practice it in moderation if pitta is aggravated.

Bellows breathing is also helpful if you want to lose some weight. Doing a few rounds of this each day will help improve your digestive power and increase your metabolism. You shouldn't do this breathing practice right before going to bed or within a couple of hours of bed, as it could invigorate the mind and cause difficulties falling asleep. But when you need a boost of energy, try this out. Other benefits of this breathing technique include:

- Promotes vitality and vigor in the body and mind
- Induces a sense of focus, peace, and tranquility
- Strengthens and balances the nervous system
- Supports proper elimination
- Improves circulation

- Cleanses the nasal passages, chest, and sinuses of excess mucus
- Alleviates asthma and allergies
- Cleanses and invigorates the spleen, liver, and pancreas
- Kindles digestive fire and tones the digestive system
- Facilitates the proper removal of carbon dioxide
- Infuses the blood with oxygen
- Strengthens the lungs and heart
- Tones the muscles of the abdomen, diaphragm, bronchial tree, and heart
- Increases lung capacity
- Cleanses and rejuvenates the lungs
- Burns toxins
- Balances excess Kapha, Vata, and pitta

This is a bit of an advanced technique, so make sure you are familiar with abdominal breathing. The instructions are meant to provide a safe, general introduction to this breath.

To perform Bellows Breath:

1. Choose a comfortable position. Cross-legged on the floor is best, using a blanket or cushion to raise the hips gently. You can also sit in a chair with your feet flat.

2. Ensure that you are sitting upright with your shoulders relaxed. Take several full breaths in through your nose. Let your hands rest on your knees. Every time you inhale, allow your belly to expand fully. Allow the eyes to close once your feel comfortable doing so.

3. You can start out by practicing the full yogic breath cycle we talked about earlier to awaken the prana maya kosha.

4. To begin your bhastrika, take an inhale in following the full yogic breath method, and then forcefully exhale without creating tension or strain. As you breathe out, let the stomach dynamically contract, pulling the belly button into the spine as the diaphragm moves towards the lungs.

5. This exhale will be followed by a forceful inhale, without tension or strain. The inhale let the stomach actively expand, pulling the belly button away from the spine and letting the diaphragm drop towards the pelvic floor.

6. Follow this with another forcefully exhale. Focus on your breath in and out, keeping the length of the breaths equal.

7. You what to make sure that the breath is controlled and originates from your diaphragm. You want to ensure that your shoulders, chest, neck, and head remain still and that the only thing moving is your belly.

Your first cycle should be made up of ten rounds. Once you reach ten, stop, and return to normal breathing, observing any sensations you may have in your body and mind. Give yourself about 15 to 30 seconds of regular breathing, and then start your next round. This one will be 20 breaths. Again, stop for 30 seconds of regular breathing, and do one last round with 30 breaths.

If you would like to add in the power of hand positions in your practice, before you begin your bellows breath, make a fist with your hands, and hold your fists next to your shoulders.

When you first start practicing this, keep the breaths relatively slow but forceful. Aim for about one breath every two seconds, and make sure you rest between rounds. With more practice, your ab muscles will become stronger, which will allow you to build up to five rounds.

Always listen to your body when you are practicing this. Bellows breathing is safe, but if you start to feel light-headed, pause for a bit and breathe naturally. Once the discomfort goes away, try another round, but keep it slower and less intense.

Bellows breath is best practiced as soon as your get up. Since this helps energize your body, doing this first thing will help wake up your body and get your blood pumping.

You can also use it to help you get through your midday slump. The midday slump normally hits right after lunch, making it hard to make it through the rest of the day. Go to a quiet place where nobody will bother you, and practice a couple of rounds of bellows breath to wake you up instead of going for some espresso.

This is also a great breathing practice to use right before a workout. It will help to warm the body and get you focused on your workout.

You should avoid this breathing technique if you are currently pregnant or menstruating. If you have uncontrolled panic disorder, seizures, epilepsy, or hypertension, or suffers from nosebleeds, glaucoma, detached retina, or recent abdominal surgery. You shouldn't do this if you have just eaten.

Dosha-Changing Pranayamas

Each pranayama practice will have a different effect on the mind-body system. Ayurveda teaches you which exercises work best for different people. Nadi Shodana, also known as alternate nostril breathing, has your alternate your breath through your left and right nostrils. This has a direct connection with the brain. When breathing through the left nostril affects the brain's right hemisphere and the right nostril with the left.

Everybody has nostril dominance, which means that we mostly breathe through that nostril. However, throughout the day, that dominance can change. Pranayama can help equalize this, but this is also why it's important to work with your Dosha.

The following practices will affect your dosha. There are three doshas, Vata, Kapha, and pitta. These are energies that live in all of us, but we all have a dominant dosha type.

Pitta is an intense and fiery type that will enjoy an occasional power trip. They can devour a mountain of food and are ready to eat again in just a few short hours.

Veta is a delicate type and can never seem to get warm. They may graze, nibble, or snack their way through the day, often feel like they need to rest. They also like talking about various diverse subjects, likely repeating themselves more than once.

Kapha is a contented type, and with thorough deliberation, eat three pieces of cake. They liked to spend time curled up on the couch making calls to their loved ones with motherly and uplifting advice.

Doshas play a dynamic role in life, constantly changing with stress, weather, and conditions. Your tendencies, whether bad or good, are caused by your doshas. You could be inclined to overeat ice cream, talk too much on the phone, or neglect sleep when you need it the most. The habits you have can influence you in positive or negative ways.

With the following pranayama techniques, you can balance out or change your dosha when you need.

Surya Bhedana

Surya Bhedana is a warming pranayam and focuses only on the right nostril. Surya, meaning sun, refers to your right nostril. This nostril is connected to the Pingala nodi. Bhedana means to pass through or pierce. When you close the nostril and force your prana to pass through only one side, you will achieve a warming effect in the body. This can help to correct an imbalance in coolness, which is common if you have a vata or Kapha dosha.

The average person will experience a conflict in their warming and cooling energies, leading to disease. This breath works in conjunction with the Chandra Bhedana, which we will go over next, to help balance out the body.

1. Start by getting into a comfortable seated position so that your spine and neck are aligned.

2. Allow your eyes to close and bring your attention to your third eye, at the space between your eyebrows.

3. Start to notice your breath and take the time to breathe deeply for a few counts, allowing your lungs to fill, and expanding your abdomen on the inhale, and contracting when you exhale.

4. Let your left arm relax in your lap or by your side. Take the right hand, and use the ring finger to block the left nostril. Your first two fingers should be folded into your palm.

5. Inhale deeply and slowly using only the right nostril.

6. Retain your breath for a moment. If you have high blood pressure or hypertension, do not hold the breath.

7. Open the left nostril and close the right using the thumb, and slowly exhale.

8. Repeat breathing in through the right nostril and breathing out through the left for one to three minutes.

9. Once you are done, allow your right arm to rest in your lap or at your side, and take a few regular breaths before opening your eyes.

If you have heart disease or high blood pressure, you may want to skip this practice. If you plan on using Surya Bhedana and Chandra Bhedana, you should not practice both on the same day.

Chandra Bhedana

Chandra is the opposite of Surya. Chandra means moon. The left nostril is used for the breath in and the right nostril for the breath out. With this breathing practice, the energy will pass through the Ida Nadi. This is associated with the cooling aspects of the body and stimulates the parasympathetic nervous system.

Practicing Chandra Bhedana helps to reduce body heat. This is effective for people with high blood pressure and can help reduce fevers. It helps to steady the mind and reduces stress, tension, and other mental problems.

1. Start by getting into a comfortable seated position. You want your spine and neck in alignment and your torso free so that you can freely breathe.

2. You will use the left hand for this practice, holding as you did in Surya Bhandana, with the index and middle finger folded against the palm, the thumb close to the left nostril, and the ring finger close to the right.

3. Before you start, decide on your inhale, hold, exhale ratio. In classic yogic texts, they say to use a 1:4:2 ratio. This could mean inhaling for two seconds, holding for eight seconds, and breathing out for four seconds. For beginners, it's advised you stick to a 1:1 ratio and skip the holding.

4. Allow your eyes to close, and then begin your practice.

5. Using ring finger, close the right nostril and breathe in.

6. Hold the breath for a moment, and then open the right nostril and close the left with your thumb. Slowly steadily release your breath.

7. Repeat this process for one to three minutes.

Avoid practicing Chandra Bhedana during the cold winter months or if you have a cold since it increases the cooling in your body. Also, people with epilepsy or low blood pressure should be very cautious if they decide to practice this.

Shitali

Shitali, sometimes spelled as sheetali, is known as cooling breath. This is a breathing practice that helps to cool the emotions, body, and mind. This comes from the Sanskrit root word sheet, which translates to "frigid" or "cold." Sheetal translates to "that which is calm, passionless, and soothing." This pranayama practice helps to calm and soothe the body-mind connection by activating an evaporative, cooling mechanism when you inhale. This provides gentle cooling energy to the tissues in your body. Amazingly, this practice will also kindle a digestive fire, just like a lump of live coal that is covered with ash can start to glow under the influence of a cold gush of wind.

Practicing shitali can help when you are in hot weather, experiencing a heated emotional situation, hot flashes, prolonged exposure to the sun, intense physical exertion, or other heat-causing circumstances. This can be a very balancing practice for pitta and is neutral toward Kapha and Vata. Nevertheless, you should practice this with care if you have an internal excess of cold or if you are experiencing especially cold weather. In this situation, you must figure out if shitali is the best pranayama for you to practice at that moment. If it is, consider balancing this practice with heating pranayama, like bhastrika.

The benefits of practicing shitali are:

- Lowers blood pressure
- Quells excess thirst
- Alleviates excess hunger
- Enhances immunity
- Sooths colicky pain
- Reduces fever
- Fosters a sense of satisfaction
- Improves the flow of prana in the body

- Soothes and calms the mind, supporting mental tranquility
- Helps to calm inflammation
- Soothes inflammatory skin conditions
- Mitigates hyper acidity in the digestive tract
- Kindles a digestive fire and improves digestion
- Cools the body and gets rid of excess heat
- Balances excess pitta

Before you start this practice, shitali requires you to roll your tongue by curling the edges up to create a tube. If you can't do this, there is an alternate version of this known as sitkari. We will go over that in the next section.

People with respiratory disorders like excessive mucus, bronchitis, or asthma, and those with low blood pressure should avoid this practice. People with chronic constipation may want to avoid this as well. Those who have heart disease can do this but don't perform the breath retention. Since the practice requires you to inhale through the mouth, which doesn't filter things like the nasal passages, you should avoid practicing heavy environmental pollution.

1. Like other pranayama techniques, this should be done on an empty stomach. Come into a comfortable seated position. Sitting cross-legged on the floor with your hips raised slightly with a blanket or pillow is best. If that's not comfortable, you can sit in a chair; just make sure you keep your feet flat on the floor.

2. Allow your hands to come to rest on your knees, and let your spine lengthen so that the head, neck, and back are erect, with the abdomen and chest open.

3. Allow your eyes to close and breathe through the nose.

4. Allow the body to relax, and practice a few rounds of full yogic breaths.

5. Once you are ready, start to work with the cooling breath.

6. Stick out your tongue and roll the edges up to form a tube. Breathe in through your curled tongue, as if you were breathing in through a straw.

7. When you breathe in, do it in the same manner as you would with a full yogic

breath, filling the lower abdomen, mid-torso, and chest, noticing the cooling effects of the air.

8. At the top of your breath, bring the tongue back in, close your mouth, and then hold your breath for a few moments. A couple of seconds is fine. You can build up the amount of time you hold your breath.

9. Then slowly release the breath through your nostrils. This is one round of cooling breath.

Do this for seven rounds. If you want to have a longer practice, you can slowly work your way up to 15 rounds. Once you are ready to bring your practice to an end, relax and breathe in and out through your nose. Let your breath come back to normal. Take some time to observe how you feel. How do you feel physically? Do you feel cooler? What sensations do you feel? Quietly observe your mind and thoughts. Once you are ready, you can open your eyes and bring awareness to everything around you.

Sitkari

Sitkari is the same pranayama practice as shitaki, except it is modified for those who can't roll their tongue. About a third of the population is genetically unable to roll their tongues into a tube. Sitkari means "hiss" or "sip." With this practice, you will be breathing through your mouth with closed teeth, which will cause a hissing noise. The benefits of sitkari are the same as above, as is the rest of the practice.

Follow the steps above until you get to the step that says to curl your tongue. Instead, you will stick out your tongue and flatten it. Gently catch your tongue between your teeth, letting the lips part and widen a bit, as if you were smiling. Inhale, and let the breath pass over the sides of your tongue and through the mouth. Follow the rest of the steps from above, completing seven rounds of sitkari breath.

The same precautions for sitali should be considered for sitkari as well. It's also advisable to make sure that the breath you are taking in is close to body temperature since your nostrils will not warm your breath. That means if you are outside at it is quite cold; you don't want to breathe that air in because it can irritate the lungs.

Ujjayi Kumbhaka

The ujjayi pranayama practice helps to calm the mind and warm the body. With this practice, you will completely fill the lungs as you contract the throat slightly and breathe in through the nose. This is a breathing technique that is commonly used in vinyasa and ashtanga yoga practices.

It comes from the Sanskrit word ujjayi, meaning "to be victorious" or "to conquer." This is why you will sometimes hear it called "victorious breath." When performed correctly, it will make a sound that is similar to the swishing of the waves in the ocean, leading to its other name of "ocean breath."

Keeping a rhythmic, steady breath is one of the most important things in yoga. When you control your breath, you can calm the mind and bring your attention to the present. This type of awareness is at the heart of yoga. Yoga teaches that if you consciously practice breath control, you can bring about positive changes in your spiritual, emotional, mental, and physical wellbeing.

Unlike several other pranayamas that are done while lying down or seated, ujjayi is often performed throughout your yoga practice in each pose. The depth, sound, and steadiness of the ujjayi breath help connect the spirit, mind, and body with the present. This unification will provide depth and richness to your yoga practice.

When you regularly practice ujjayi, you can release pent-up emotions. The added oxygen and deep exhales will strengthen and invigorate your physical practice. It is beneficial in calming your mind. It can also help those who suffer from mental tension, insomnia, and stress. With time, you will learn the best way to guide the breath so that the breath can guide your practice.

As you practice ujjayi, make sure you don't tighten the throat. Be very careful if you have a respiratory problem like emphysema or asthma. Stop immediately if you start feeling dizzy or faint. Ensure that you are always working with your abilities and limits, and don't push yourself beyond those limits. These practices are meant to help, not harm you. If you have any concerns medically, speak with a doctor before you start practicing this.

Start by getting in a comfortable seated position. Relax the body and let your eyes close. Allow your mouth to drop open a bit, and relax your tongue and jaw

Breathe in and out deeply through your mouth. Feel as the air passes through your throat as you breathe in.

When you release the breath, slightly contact the back of the throat, like you do when you whisper. Softly whisper "ahh," as you breathe out. If it helps, imagine that you are trying to fog up the window.
As you get more comfortable with how the exhales feel, maintain that constriction when you breathe in as well. You will start to hear your breath making an ocean sound.

Once you have comfortable control of your breath, let your mouth close and perform the breath solely through the nose. Make sure you maintain the same constriction in the throat as you had when the mouth was open. You should continue to hear the same sound. Direct your breath over the vocal cords and the back of the throat. Your mouth should remain closed with the lips soft.

Keep your concentration on the sound of your breath. Let this sound soothe the mind. You should be able to hear the breath, but a person standing several feet away should not be able to hear it.

Make sure your inhales fill the lungs completely and fully release that air when you breathe out.

Start out practicing this for five minutes. You can increase the time up to 15 minutes. You can start to link your breath to your movement gradually. When you use ujjayi with asanas, inhale as you extend and expand, and exhale when you fold and contract.

The most common mistake made with this breath is tightening the throat. There should only be a slight constriction. As you become more familiar with this, you can use it during any yoga session without pausing. You can also ask your yoga teacher for feedback on whether you are doing it right or need a modification. Advanced practitioners can again try other variations with proper instructions. You can use bandhas, or muscular locks, like the throat lock, but only once you have practiced this sufficiently.

Kapalbhati

Kapalbhati is considered an intermediate-advanced practice made up of powerful and short exhales followed by a passive inhale. This practice is done to help purify your body and help tone and cleanse the respiratory system. This is done by encouraging your body to release waste and toxins. It can help to leave your mind and body rejuvenated and refreshed.

When you practice pranayama, 80% of your toxins are released through your exhale. Regularly practicing kapalbhati helps to detoxify the body. The most obvious sign of a healthy body is to have a shining forehead.

Broken down, kapalbhati is made up of two Sanskrit words, "kapala," meaning skull, and "bhati," meaning light. This is why it is sometimes called "skull brightener breath" or "light skull breathing." As you perform this, you can picture the area around the skull filling with the light of enlightenment. You have likely heard of the breath of fire, and this is that such practice.

Kapalabhati is warming and invigorating. It cleanses the respiratory system, lungs, and sinuses, which can prevent allergies and illnesses. Regularly practicing this helps to strengthen the abdominal muscles and diaphragm. This exercise can also help increase your oxygen, energize and stimulate the brain, which will help you get ready for your meditation and anything else that will require you to focus. Other benefits are:

- Uplifts and calms the mind
- It energizes your nervous system and helps rejuvenate the brain
- It helps trim and tighten the belly
- Improves digestive tract functioning, assimilation, and absorption of nutrients
- Improves blood circulation and brings an extra radiance to the face
- Stimulates the abdominal organs, which makes it helpful for those who have diabetes
- Clears the nadis

- Increases your metabolic rate, aiding in weight loss

Kapalabhati is an advanced technique. Don't try to do this if you aren't proficient with the basic breathing techniques. Avoid practicing this if you have heart disease, a hernia, or high blood pressure. Pregnant women should avoid this, as well. Approach this with caution if you have any type of respiratory condition, like emphysema or asthma.

You should stop the exercise if you start to feel dizzy or faint. Make sure you work with your abilities and limits.

1. To get started, come into a comfortable seated position where you can keep your spine straight and your abdomen free. If sitting on the floor is not comfortable for you, you can also sit in a chair; just make sure that you keep your feet on the floor and back straight.

2. Allow your hands to rest, palms down, on your knees.

3. Start focusing on the lower abdomen. You can also place your hands, one over the other, on your lower abdomen.

4. Take a deep breath in through your nose.

5. Contract the low abdomen. You can also use your hands and press into the area, forcing your breath out in a short burst.

6. Release this contraction quickly to allow in a passive and automatic inhale. You need to keep your focus only on the exhale. All will be passive.

7. Start this slowly, aiming for about 65 to 70 contractions each minute. Gradually speed up the pace where you can get to 95 to 105 cycles each minute. Make sure you stick to your own pace, and always stop if you ever start to feel dizzy or faint.

8. After a minute of this, take a deep breath in through the nose and slowly breathe out through the mouth. Depending on how experienced you are, you can do this for another round.

If this practice is performed correctly, you will start feeling invigorated, energized, and cleansed. This practice will require knowledge and experience with the basic techniques. Make sure, if you are new to this, that you get used to ujjayi first. Plus, it would help if you remember the following things as you do this:

- If your breath ever starts feeling strained or feel anxious or dizzy, stop, and breathe regularly.
- Don't force your breath on the inhale or the exhale.
- Keep your shoulders and spine still during this exercise. The only thing that should move is your lower belly.
- Your abdomen should not be contracted when you inhale.
- Stay focused on your lower abdomen, and your exhales.

Some other precautions for this pranayama technique include those who have an artificial pacemaker or stent, backache caused by a slipped disc, hernia, epilepsy, or have recently had abdominal surgery. Women should avoid this if they are pregnant or just gave birth and during menstruation.

Sama Vritti

Sama vritti pranayama translates to equal or the same fluctuations. When practiced, it requires a steady exhale and inhale that has an equal duration. This pattern of breathing helps to soothe the body and mind. If you start feeling anxious, disconnected, or overwhelmed, this breath teaches you to support and steady the gentle shift of your parasympathetic nervous system. It can help to stabilize and ground an overactive Vata so that the body and mind can relax.

Sama vritti is commonly used in asana practice. By learning how to do this in a seated practice, you will improve your ability to flow through your movements with a better connection and steady breath.

- Start by getting into a comfortable seated position with the hips elevated on a blanket or pillow. You can sit in a chair and keep your feet flat on the floor. This helps to support the diaphragm to allow your breath to come easier. You can also do this while lying down.

- As you get settled, start noticing your natural breath pattern. Notice how long the breaths are and the sensations that you have in your body. Notice how you transition from your inhale to your exhale. If you have tension, see how you can change it to smooth it and release the transitions' tension.

- Then begin to count the inhale. Take a deep breath in for a count of four. Begin the exhale, breathing out for a four-count. Repeat this for a few rounds.

- If the count of four seems too short, you can slowly start to increase the count, working up to ten. The main thing is to keep the count the same for the inhale and exhale. Keep the count at a number that is comfortable for you.

- You should do ten rounds of this breath, keeping a gentle pace. Continue to relax and stay in the present moment. If you end up losing count, start over again.

- As you bring your practice to a close, allow the breath to go back to normal. Notice any peaceful changes you feel in your body and mind.

You can add retentions at the top of the breath, holding it for the same count as breathing in and out. If you are new to this, you can leave the retentions out if they are uncomfortable. You can also keep the retentions shorter if you need to. It's more important that your breath in and out is the same.

Make sure you never strain or force your breath when practicing this or any other pranayama technique. If you are pregnant, you can do this breathing technique; just drop the retentions. People with ear, eye, heart, or lung problems or high blood pressure should not hold the breath. If you have low blood pressure, don't hold your breath after the exhale.

There are many other pranayama techniques, but these are the most commonly used techniques and provide you with lots of benefits. For beginners, go slow and start with simple techniques until you get used to the feel of deep belly breaths.

Chapter 4: The Yogi's Diet

The practice of yoga also has suggestions for your life, such as your diet and sex. This section will go over some important lifestyle choices that you should consider to lead a healthy life.

Sexuality and How It Affects Your Life

In today's modern cultures, especially in the West, when a person thinks about sexuality and yoga, it normally brings up images of celibate monks walking around in their orange robes. Or they think of the total opposite, which would be tantric sex that promises its participants they will reach high levels of consciousness, but this might seem a bit tawdry to some. What does yoga actually say about sex?

According to yoga, sex is a sacred act involving two souls that merge and blend into one. It is an experience that is not ordinary, where our souls transcend, dance with the polarities, and then merge into one like in Tantra. This is one of the closest experiences you will have with infinity.

If you look up "sex" in the dictionary, you might find a definition that says something like: "sexual union that involved penetrating a vagina by a penis." This describes sex as a physical act, but it doesn't include any of the above things. This is simply basic sex.
Sex has a Greek root that means "separation," which reinforces a distinction between two people. Yoga is to total opposite of sex. Yoga's definition is "to get rid of separation or to yoke." Yoga is considered to be a Tantric practice. Tantra comes from a Sanskrit word that simply means to "tan" or stretch and "tra" across. The English words for traverse and travel come from the same root word, "tra." Tantra is actually referring to being able to stretch your perception of others and yourself or to stretch across the chasm that divides all people from one another.

In the Patanjali sutras, it explains how sexual energy is very potent. When it gets directed to the higher Chakras, it could lead to a more enlightened state of being. Semen is known as "ojas," and it was not to be wasted. Semen isn't just a sexual fluid but a lubricant for the nervous system and brain. According to yoga theories, it takes 80 bites of food to make just one drop of blood, and 80 drops of blood make a drop of semen.

In the West, most people's attitudes about yoga were influenced by Shankaracharya, who taught Vedanta during the eighth century and caused the sannyasin movement. These were the celibate monks, wore the orange robes, and turned away from the ways of the world. Another teacher from the 1500s, Vallabhacharya, taught people the only way to reach God was through the world's activities. The people who hold this lineage were married. These monks were trying to reach these higher states of being.

As it was explained in the Hatha Yoga Pradipika and the Patanjali's Yoga Sutra, Yoga didn't have a negative view of the world. Still, it does say that yoga looks at an ignorant mind or an unpurified body as an obstacle that will keep them from reaching enlightenment.

Yoga gives a person ways to practice to master their own body and minds to purify their body and overcome all their negative, past, karmic tendencies. Yoga can transform our bodies into instruments that could be used to tap into or access more knowledge that could then lead to the moksha-liberation from samsara or the cycle of birth, life, and death.

The Yogi Bhajan told his students only to have sex one time each month. Yes, you read that right. He said it was very important to preserve a man's "ojas." If this can be done, one can raise the Kundalini energy. He also said that sex begins three days before you actually have intercourse. This is what used to be known as "courtship." It was best for the woman to be in a place where she could feel safe, secure and where the couple can go to sleep afterward. You can get this place ready for her by lighting some candles, using aromatherapy, and anything else you know of that will put her mind and body at ease.

A person's sexual experiences can become imprinted in their subconscious mind and their aura. Every one of them will be interwoven with a different intensity. Being too much of a flirt can make holes in your aura, too.

Bhajan's teachings say that women have two arc lines. The first one runs from one ear to the other and is called the Halo. This one's color will depend on their mental and physical health. The other ones are running from nipple to nipple. This one will get imprinted with all the sexual experiences that they have had in their life. A woman needs to clear these energies to keep their aura clear and strong. A woman's energy is super sensitive. Electromagnetic fields can have a very destructive effect on them. They can become extremely weak emotionally. If her relationships are based on respect, trust, and love, she can flourish and be expansive, vital, secure, and creative.

A person's intention can bring about any action's result. This means if you want to purify your actions, you have to have a pure intention. A person might decide to engage in sex for selfish reasons, such as wanting to dominate or humiliate their partner. Another person has sex with another to uplift and cherishes them. Some people might describe the first one as "rape," whereas the second one might be considered an act of "making love." They are both the same act, but each was done with extremely different intentions.

Take a minute and think about the energy we waste, either unconsciously or consciously, due to sex, how we dress, how we act, our buying preferences, our sexual preferences, how we look, and so on.
Take a few moments and think about how your life would be different if sex weren't in the picture, you might then realize just how large a role sex plays in your life.

Spirituality and sexuality used not to go together, but now spiritual practices are getting larger in every form, and more people are bringing more meaning into their sexual experiences. Sex is a wonderful union, but it could also be sacred.

Let's get back to Tantric sex for a minute. The main use for Tantra is to give two people faces so they can see each other as people. If you take time to look into another person's eyes, you are going to see yourself. This is the main teaching of yoga. It is known as shunyata or emptiness. This basically means that everybody we meet is actually coming from ourselves. You could say these are essences that are coming up from our past karma. If you are having sex with another person and you took time to look deeply into their face, to get completely naked and I'm not just talking physically naked but spiritually naked, it could take the sexiness out of the moment.

One good benefit of Tantric sex is that it can cleanse the subconscious mind. During the process, painful or forgotten memories could come to the surface, and they might feel emotional lows and highs. They might be feeling happy, and then suddenly they become very sad, begins crying, and they don't know why. Once you realize why this happens, you can look at your partner in a whole new light.

Love can be scary. When you are in love, there aren't any other faces or bodies because the two of you merge into one transcendental body. In this vastness of being, there isn't a lot of space for bodies, and this is why most people have sex just for the fun of it.

You can achieve enlightened sex, but it will be extremely rare. For people who are just interested in reaching enlightenment, celibacy is probably your best option. You should not encourage celibacy if it isn't your own decision. If you make this commitment just because someone else said it was the right thing to do or it will make you pure and holy, it will only lead to suffering and trouble, and it won't last.

Brahmacharya, which can be translated to celibacy, is a practice that Patanjali recommends. For many people, this means you have to abstain from sex. Brahma means God, and charya refers to a vehicle that can take you places, so brahmacharya means "to use sex with the intention of moving toward God." You could reword it to "moving toward Yoga."

The way we look at sex now came from when we began domesticating animals, which involved breeding them, and one might have had to manipulate them sexually. Animal industries don't think about the animals with regards to their well being or happiness. They are only looked at as objects to be abused sexually and then killed for consumption. This connection between sex and killing should tell you all you need to know about our way of life. When the majority of our economy is based on abusing animals sexually and killing them for profit, this affects the way our intimate encounters go with other humans. If you aren't connected, you aren't going to have any intimacy.

Humans have compartmentalized sex as another function or another responsibility that we have to do, and most of the time, it happens without love or compassion. We have been told that our bodies are different from our spirit and mind. This means that we have divided our spiritual being from our physical being.

How can we move sex from something that was exploited into recognizing another human as something more than just their genitalia and what they can do for us? It starts with the question: "What can they do for me?" We have to change that into: "What could I do for them?" "Is there a way I can enhance their life?" "What could I do to make them feel cherished, happier, or better?"

This all starts with looking them in the face and asking: "Who are you?" "Who am I?" "Who are we?" "What are we doing?" "Why are we doing it?" All of these are very powerful questions.

All the things we see in the world are a projection of what's inside all of us. Yoga is a connection, whereas sex can be a separation. Yoga allows you to see yourself in others. It lets you see them so deeply that they disappear, and you become one. When this happens, sex goes away, but the oneness stays. This is what love is all about.

Why You Need To Eat Right

Our mental and physical well-being depends on the things we eat, the way we eat, and the amount of food we eat. Mitahara is one of the Yamas in ancient Indian traditions. Mita simply means "moderate," and ahara means "diet." So to put it simply, mitahara would mean to eat a moderate diet.

It is recommended that you only eat when you feel hungry. When you see sweet food, it isn't referring to sugary foods, and it means pleasant tasting, fresh foods. Offering part of your food to Shiva means that you should eat food to nourish your body to be a source of spirituality.

Yoga doesn't put foods into groups like fats, proteins, and carbohydrates. It puts them in groups like Taamsik, Raajsik, and Saatvic according to how they can affect the mind and body. Tamasic foods are ones that make you feel sluggish or lethargic. Raajsik foods will bring restlessness and activity. Sattvic foods will make you feel enthusiastic, energetic, and light.
Some foods need to be avoided at all costs. These are called Apathy. There are some foods that you can eat, and these are called Pathya.

It isn't healthy to eat foods that have been reheated once they have gotten cold. It isn't healthy to eat foods that don't have any natural oils in them or have been dried. It isn't healthy to eat foods that are too acidic, salty, or stale.

A healthy diet will include pure water, some vegetables, cucumbers, dry ginger, honey, crystallized sugar, brown sugar, ghee, milk, barley, rice, wheat, and grains.

The most important thing about a diet is that it needs to nourish the seven dhatus: the ova or semen, fat, marrow, bone, blood, flesh, and skin. Any foods that destroy the body's natural balance shouldn't be eaten.
The right types of food aren't all we need. We have to know the right amount of food to eat and when to eat it. Our bodies can help us know when we have reached the limit of food we need to eat. If we can listen to our bodies attentively and learn to eat mindfully, we will know when to stop. We should never waste Prana on digestion.

Having a happy and pleasant state of mind while cooking and eating could help keep Prana in your food. One should never eat too much or too little. You should never sleep too little or too much.

Yoga is a practice that can bring the body and mind together and stops all our mental wanderings. Diet is an important part of human existence and yoga. When talking about Indian philosophy, the diet is thought of as being a sacred entity. A person grows from the food that they eat. Shrimadbhagvad Gita considers a diet as one that is balanced.

A diet that completely encompasses Yoga practices is called a Yogic diet. According to their philosophy, most of the foods we eat nourish the skin where the subtle parts of food will nourish the other parts of the body. If you want to raise your consciousness, you need to purify the outer sheath by following a prescribed diet mentioned in the Yogic Scriptures. These scriptures tell about timing, quantity, and quality, and the order of eating food.

Diet plays an important role in having success when practicing Yoga. If you want to have success, you have to begin with choosing the right foods. Eating the right foods is essential before practicing pranayama.
If you practice yoga without controlling your diet, you will suffer from several diseases and won't progress. If your fun and food are well balanced, your actions and movements will be balanced, your waking and sleeping will be balanced, and your yoga will get rid of all your sorrows.

There are three types of diets: Tamasic, Rajasic, and Sattvic. Everybody will have three qualities that help decide the likings and nature of others. People who have three qualities will have three food types. The Shri Krishna places their diet into three categories.

Tamasic Diet

This diet contains foods that are very heavy and can cause lethargy or fatigue. These foods need to be avoided at all costs, especially if you suffer from depression or any chronic ailment. Tamasic foods include unripe fruits, overripe fruits, rotten foods, stale foods, alcohol, red meat, processed foods, deep-fried foods, burned foods, or fermented foods.

Rajasic Diet

These foods should be refrained from and include: any caffeinated drink, overly processed foods, artificial additives, spicy foods, any foods that irritate the mucus membranes, mushrooms, onions, garlic, etc.

Sattvic Diet

This diet uses food in its natural state. Foods that are fresh and don't have any preservatives or additives. These foods need to be eaten in their natural form it at all possible, for example, raw, lightly cooked, or steamed. This diet comprises fresh vegetables and fruit, whole grains, nuts, lentils, pulses, seeds, natural sweeteners like honey, and herbs.

Sleep Quality

Sleep is needed for your well-being and health, but millions of people don't get the right amount of sleep, and most of these suffer from this. Some studies have shown that more than 40 million Americans have 70 various sleep disorders, and 60% of all the adults who were asked said they have problems sleeping a couple of nights every week.

Many of these have gone untreated and undiagnosed. Over 40 percent of the adults asked to say they experience daytime sleepiness that is so severe it interferes with their daily lives. About 69 percent of children have experienced some sleep problems a couple of nights each week.

Sleep is just as needed as eating a healthy diet and getting regular exercise. Today's living doesn't always embrace the need for sleep, but it is just as important to our health. We have to make an effort to get regular sleep. Here are some benefits that are associated with getting enough sleep:

Better Concentration and Productivity

Many studies have been done that looked at what sleep deprivation can do to our bodies. Researchers concluded sleep was lined to some brain functions, including:

- Cognition
- Productivity
- Concentration

A study done in 2015 showed children's sleep patterns could impact their academic performance and behaviors.

Low Weight Gain

There seems to be a link between short sleep patterns, obesity, and weight gain, but it isn't completely clear. Many studies have been done that have linked poor sleep with obesity.

Another study that was done recently says that there isn't a link between sleep deprivation and being overweight. This research argues that other studies didn't take into account other factors like:

- Long sedentary time
- Long hours at work
- Level of education

- Physical activity
- Having type 2 diabetes
- Alcohol consumption

Not getting enough sleep can affect someone's ability or desire to maintain a healthy lifestyle, but it might or might not contribute to weight gain.

Calorie Regulation

This is similar to weight gain, but this suggests that getting enough sleep could help a person eat fewer calories when awake. One study concluded that sleep patterns could affect a person's hormones that are responsible for appetite.

If you don't get enough sleep, it might interfere with your body's ability to regulate your food intake correctly.

Better Athletic Ability

The National Sleep Foundation says the right amount of sleep for adults is between seven to nine hours each night. Athletes could benefit from getting ten hours of sleep nightly. Sleep is just as important to athletes as eating the right amount of calories and getting the right nutrients.

The main reason behind this is our bodies heal while it sleeps. Some other benefits might include:

- Functioning better mentally
- Faster
- More coordination
- Better energy
- Better performance

Heart Disease Risk Lowered

The main risk factor for getting heart disease is high blood pressure. Getting the right amount of sleep every night lets our body's blood pressure regulate itself. Doing this could reduce the chances of conditions like apnea and promote overall better heart health.

More Emotional and Social Intelligence

Sleep has been linked to a person's social and emotional intelligence. If you don't get the right amount of sleep, you might have more issues seeing other people's expressions and emotions.

One study looked at a person's responses to different emotional stimuli. They concluded that a person's empathy wasn't as strong when they didn't get enough sleep.

Prevents Depression

The association between mental health and sleep has been studied for a very long time. One conclusion was there is a link between depression and sleep deprivation. Another study looked at patterns of suicides for ten years. It concluded that not getting enough sleep was a contributing factor to most of those deaths.

Other studies said that people who had sleep problems like insomnia showed greater signs of depression.

Lowered Inflammation

A link has been found between getting enough sleep and lowering the body's inflammation. One study suggests there is a link between inflammatory bowel disease and sleep deprivation. This study showed that not getting enough sleep contributed to these diseases, and these diseases can cause sleep deprivation.

Better Immune System

Sleep can help our bodies recover, regenerate, and repair. Our immune system isn't an exception. Research has shown that getter better sleep could help our bodies fight off infections. Scientist still has to do more research to find the exact sleep mechanisms regarding its impact on our immune system.

Signs of Excessive Sleepiness

Moodiness, irritability, and disinhibition are the first signs of sleep deprivation. If you don't get enough sleep after these first few signs, you might begin experiencing impaired memory, multitasking ability, flattened emotional responses, slowed speech, or not being able to original. As you start falling asleep, you might fall into what is known as microsleep that can cause their attention to lapse, or they might nod off while reading or driving, and then they might begin having hallucinations at the beginning of REM sleep.

Sleep Problem Causes

People who study sleep disorders discovered that issues within the following systems could indirectly or directly cause these problems:

- Immune
- Metabolic functions
- Cardiovascular
- Nervous
- Brain

Other diseases, disorders, and unhealthy conditions could cause sleep issues, including:

- Drug abuse
- Alcohol abuse
- Diabetes
- Metabolic syndrome
- Obesity
- Emotional disorders like bipolar disorder or depression
- Elevated cardiovascular risks like stroke or MI
- Hypertension
- Pathological sleepiness
- Accidents
- Insomnia

People who are at more of a risk for lack of sleep might include teenagers, parents, truck drivers, physicians, and night shift workers.

Ways Behavior and Environment Affects Sleep

Stress is the main cause of sleeping problems. Most triggers include pressures at work or school, marriage problems, family problems, death, or serious illness. Normally the problem will go away when the stress goes away. If sleep problems, like insomnia, aren't dealt with, they can continue even once the stressor has gone away.

Environmental factors like a room's temperature, noise levels, or brightness level can hamper a sound sleep. Interruptions from family members or children can hinder sleep, too. You need to pay attention to the size of your bed, the comfort of your mattress, and your partner's sleep habits. If you sleep beside somebody who has a different sleep preference, snores, can't stay asleep, have problems falling asleep, or has other problems, it will soon become your problem, too!

Health Problems

There are a number of physical problems that can affect a person's ability to sleep. Conditions that cause pain like arthritis, discomfort, or backaches makes it hard to get a restful sleep.

Some studies suggest that sleep complaints that were reported by the patient were connected with a higher risk for cardiovascular mortality and morbidity. For women, being pregnant or experiencing shifts in hormones can hinder sleep, too.

Some medications like steroids, decongestants, and medicines for depression, asthma, or high blood pressure could cause side effects like sleep problems. It would be a good idea to speak to your doctor about any sleep problems that persist or happens for more than a couple of weeks.

A number of psychiatric disorders can cause fatigue, including bipolar disorder, seasonal affective disorder, mixed anxiety-depression, dysthymia, minor depression, or postpartum depression.

Decision Making and Sleepiness

In August of 2004, performed a study to find how sleepiness can affect risk-taking and decision making. They found that lack of sleep did take a toll on making good decisions.

The researchers asked for volunteers, and they put them into two groups. One group was sleep deprived while the other group got to sleep. They were then asked to do a series of tasks on a computer. They were told they could stop and take the money or keep going and lose all their money. If they chose to keep going and didn't finish all their work in the amount of time they had, they would lose all of their money.

The more alert people were compassionate about how much work had to be done to finish everything on time, and they understood their risk of losing money. The sleepy subjects decided to quit so they didn't lose all their money because they didn't believe they would be able to finish.

Consequences of Sleep Deprivation

Most car accidents were attributed to sleep-deprived people—falling asleep while driving has caused 100,000 car crashes, which has resulted in 1550 deaths and 71,000 injuries each year. People in their 20s or teens were involved in over half of the car crashes that occur on the highway every year. A lack of sleep can interfere with their ability to learn in school.

Some of the risk factors for sleepiness crashes:

- Medical residents driving home after their shift
- Night workers

- Commercial truck drivers
- Young adult males
- People who only get less than six hours of sleep
- Patients whose sleepiness went untreated
- Early morning or late night driving

Sleep Recommendations

A person's sleep needs are going to change from person to person. It all depends on their age. As you age, you normally require less and less sleep to function properly.

It gets broken down as follows:

- 0 to 3 months: 14 to 17 hours
- 4 to 12 months: 12 to 16 hours ·
- 1 to 2 years: 11 to 14 hours
- 3 to 5 years: 10 to 13 hours
- 6 to 12 years: 9 to 12 hours
- 13 to 18 years: 8 to 10 hours
- 18 to 60 years: 7 + hours
- 61 to 65 years: 7 to 9 hours
- 65 + years: 7 to 8 hours

Just the number of hours isn't as important as the quality of sleep you are getting. Here are some signs of poor quality of sleep:

- Not feeling rested after sleeping all night
- Waking up multiple times during the night

Here are some things you can do to improve your quality of sleep:

- Reduce stress by exercising or therapy
- Spend some time outside and be more active throughout the day
- Go to bed every night at the same time
- Don't try to sleep if you have gotten enough sleep

Ways to Get Good Sleep

Sleep researchers say that the five stages of sleep are defined by a person's brain waves, which reflect deep or light sleep. REM sleep increases in the morning. This is the time during sleep when a person dreams and the muscles are relaxed. This is also where your memories get consolidated in the brain.

Experts say the snooze button isn't going to help you feel more rested. It will diminish the rest you have gotten. This is because it affects your brain waves. It shortens the REM cycle, and this can impair their mental functions throughout the day.

Some techniques can combat sleep problems like:

- Try to go to bed earlier for a certain amount of time. This makes sure that you get enough sleep
- Try to make a point of waking up before your alarm
- Have a set bedtime
- Get rid of all lights and lessen the noise where you sleep
- Make sure the temperature in the room is comfortable
- Get some exercise
- Don't eat anything heavy before you go to bed
- Don't drink any alcoholic beverages late at night
- Don't smoke if you wake up during the night
- Don't smoke before or as you are getting ready for bed.
- Don't eat or drink anything caffeinated before going to bed
- Create and keep a regular wake and sleep schedule

Sleep is usually neglected even though it is a vital component of our overall well being and health. Sleep is needed since it helps the body repair itself so you can be ready and fit for the next day.

Getting the right amount of rest might keep us from gaining weight, keep us away from heart disease, and lessens the duration of an illness.

Four Basic Urges and Regulating Lifestyle

Creating a lifestyle that is conducive to meditation can be a bit hard to do. The word lifestyle is a vast subject. It contains many religious, social, and cultural connotations. We aren't trying to give you any rules or guidelines from any religious, social, or cultural perspective. Yoga is universal in nature and can be helpful for everyone, and it doesn't matter what their background is.

Think about an athlete who does a competition or day of endurance, but they haven't done any training. They hadn't done any prior physical exercises. There wasn't any effort to do anything relaxing before their competition. They ate foods that are loaded with salt, sugar, and fats but very low in nutrients. They stayed up all night and didn't have regular sleeping habits. Their social life and family was in chaos. They have several unexamined emotional and mental challenges.

These athletes might find with some of these areas in life, but a true athlete knows that they need balance, especially during their event.

The same thing holds true for meditators. Common sense shows us that there is a relationship between our lifestyle and being able to relax, become centered, balanced, or calm in our mind, breath, and body.

Four Basic Urges and Lifestyle

According to the psychology of yoga, there are four basic urges. These are necessities, needs, wants, or desires for:

- Self-preservation
- Sex
- Sleep
- Food

These are fountains or sources, and this isn't saying that there aren't other desires we have. These are the four at the root of most of the other ones. We could call these the "Four Primitive Fountains" since they are the fountains or sources from where all the other desires come from.

People who are in marketing know all about these. Just think about the things we see most often in ads. You will see people eating, relaxing, have romantic interactions, romantic facial expressions, and are usually focusing on problems that could be a threat to us. The service or product that is being marketed is a solution for fulfilling some of these urges.

This same holds for the movie industry. Most movies will deal with some sort of threat or challenge that they need to overcome that involves a normally set romance in a bedroom or restaurant. Even though the movie themes might seem alike, all the possibilities will bring about entertainment.

Suggesting that you need to regulate the four urges doesn't mean that you have to become impervious to them. It doesn't mean that you have to renounce them, or that you have to have a boring life. It means that you have to intelligently regulate these drives in healthy ways to move forward with your spiritual practices.

Emphasizing the Four Areas

There are other necessities, needs, desires, wishes, or wants that come from these four. There is such a small number at the center that could make the situation a lot more manageable. It won't be as hard for us to talk about and learn how to do this without judging.

There is a huge amount of diversity in the number of ways people might regulate these four urges. Exploring these four urges can help you see the entire process of managing your lifestyle a lot clearer. You can adapt this to your individual religious, social, or cultural backgrounds.

If you try to address all the different aspects of managing this lifestyle, it might seem overwhelming, just like you may never be qualified to start meditating. Having just four areas that you have to focus on could give the process simplicity.

Observing and Regulating the Four Urges

You know what the four urges are, but there are two aspects about dealing with the urges:

- You observe the functions of these urges and how they relate to the four mind functions buddhi, ahamkara, Chitta, and manas. This just means that you have to pay attention to your thoughts, speech, and actions.

- It was regulating these urges in ways that won't create obstacles for your meditation. This means that you have to make good choices.

As students try to observe their influences and regulate the urges, it will clarify how the urges are fountains where expectations, needs, wants, and desires spring forth.

You can immediately see how these four can cause emotional responses, control your thinking, and could unconsciously direct speech and actions. The latent impressions and tendencies that have been buried deep in our unconsciousness will become know during meditation.

The two factors of observation and regulation are like the question: "Which comes first, the chicken or the egg?" The truth is they both always recycle one into the other. So there will always be a cycle of chicken, egg, chicken, egg, etc. Observations and regulations could also recycle into observation, regulation, observation, regulation, observation, etc.

Having a specific degree of regulation can create an improved environment for observation. Having a more lucid observation can bring about a better regulation ability by making clear choices with more determination.

This will slowly turn into a beautiful dance between regulation and observation that will lead you toward the contentment of a mind that has been trained. You will then be capable of developing a deeper meditation.

As you progress with your meditations, you need to remember that regulation and observation do go together, just like the right foot and left foot go together when you are walking. You have been gentle and nice to yourself while you are moving forward.

Food

If you have questions about the relationship between meditation and food, just remember the large meals you have on holidays. You might have eaten more than you should have. The foods that you ate might not have been as healthy as they could have been. You can probably remember that most of these foods had a lot of spices, sugars, and fats in them, but man, they were delicious. These foods are usually processed to the point that they don't have any more nutritional values, and some chemicals have been added to them.

Think about the way you felt after you ate all that food. Did you feel heavy, stuffed, sleepy, tired? You need to answer honestly here. I know I'm always ready for a nap after a big meal. Did you ever feel like going to your sacred space and meditating? What might have happened if you had meditated after you ate that big meal?

Now, I am not saying that you can't have those large family meals, but the point I'm trying to make is this:

You know that food can change the state of mind or state of energy. You aren't going to need a swami to tell you. You don't need any clinical researchers or doctors to tell you that there are lesser and better foods. We know about food quality, even though we might not follow the wisdom that we have.

Exploring the foods that we eat could be a very complex task. There are numerous videos, books, and health programs. It isn't my intent to replicate that work or tell you that there is a perfect diet. Two principles in yoga relate to food that might be useful to remember. Then, the choices you make about food could be made in these two principles:

Cleansing and Nutrition

Food is the stuff coming in and going out of us. This process is straightforward. There are two parts to it:

- Cleansing
- Nutrition

Our bodies do a good job of cleansing themselves to a certain limit. If we give our bodies high-quality foods, our bodies will be able to process it easily and then get rid of what it doesn't need.

If we put in huge amounts of fewer quality foods, our bodies have to work harder to get rid of what it doesn't need. When our bodies have to work harder to get rid of the large volume of all that low-quality stuff, the effect is all the waste won't get removed as fast, and the body will store it as fat. This causes the body to have a high level of toxicity.

The other thing to look at is the nutrients that we are putting into our bodies. If there aren't enough nutrients coming in, then all the different systems in our bodies won't work properly. We won't feel well emotionally, mentally, or physically. You might eat huge quantities of food that is high in calories but very low in nutrients. This effect might be that you could be starving even though you are eating a lot of calories.

The two principles of nutrition and cleansing go together, and they do this very well as long as we can remember some principles. When you eat or make choices about food, just be aware of the relationship between that certain food and its nutritional value and if it is capable of cleansing the body. Now ask yourself, "Will this food be good or bad for me?" "Will it go easily through my body?"

Even if you decide to eat a food that isn't as good, you will be eating mindfully. Slowly you will improve your diet, and this will happen naturally or by using other guidance or resources.

It might be useful to read some books about nutrition or diet or take some classes about cooking healthy foods. Most yoga teachers and health food stores know where to find these classes.

Water

Giving people advice about foods can be a bit complex, but at the same time, it is very simple. During the time you are working on improving your food choices, there is one extremely simple practice that can work for everyone, and this is drinking enough water.

The recommendations about how much water to drink will vary depending on who you talk to, but at the minimum, you need to get eight glasses each day. This means you should drink about two quarts a day. Doubling this amount is a good way to keep your system clean. The best way to know if you are getting enough water is to check your urine color. When you wake each morning, your urine is going to have some
color to eat. If you notice that your urine has color to it during the day, you aren't drinking enough water. Your urine should be a very pale yellow color.

Vitamins

There are many opinions about taking vitamins. I don't intend to get into a debate about it. Even though you eat well and think you are getting all the minerals and vitamins you need in your food, you might have a "hole" in your nutrient intake. There might be one mineral or vitamin that you haven't been getting in your diet.

One way to deal with this is to take a multivitamin daily. You might want to do this for a short time and see if you feel different. If you do see a difference, you might have found that you had a "hole" in your diet. You could explore with your food to see if you can find the deficiency and when you do, you can adjust your vitamin intake to take care of the deficiency, or you could just continue with your multivitamin. You just need to be aware that there might be a "hole" in your nutrients and then handle it to the best of your ability.

Conclusion

Thank you for making it through to the end of the book. Let's hope it was informative and able to provide you with all of the tools you need to achieve your goals, whatever they may be.

The next step is to start your pranayama breathing practice. With the information you have learned, you can decide what asana you want to use and which breathing practice you want to do. The great thing is, you don't have to do the same pranayama every time. You can do various breaths, but the important thing is that you make this breathing practice something you do regularly. It's like meditation so that you can simply do these practices once a day. Remember, though, some of these can be used during times of stress to help calm you down. Do what your body tells you it needs. That also means listening to any pain you experience during your practice. That said, you shouldn't experience pain, so you will want to stop and figure out what may be going wrong if you do feel any type of pain. It could be that your position is not working for you. That means all you have to do is change the way you are sitting.

Pranayama is an important practice for anybody looking to feel good. It's fairly simple, especially once you learn the basics. Don't let the names discourage you. Anybody can practice pranayam, so get started today.

Finally, if you found this book useful in any way, a review on Amazon is always appreciated!